# empowered

Understanding the Holy Spirit in this generation

# empowered

Understanding the Holy Spirit in this generation

## CALEB WEHRLI

# contents

# foreword

**M**y knees were bowed on the sawdust floor and my face buried in my hands as music softly played in the background. I had just responded to the altar call at my first-ever youth camp service. At sixteen years of age, the message of the Holy Spirit was fresh to me. Though converted only one month earlier, my love for Jesus was growing daily and I longed to know Him in a deeper way. Bowing at the altar alone in quiet prayer, I dedicated my life anew to God's purpose and calling. My inner man stretched itself toward the eternal God as I longed for His presence, approval, and power. It was a quiet experience at first, but the altar service continued, and then throughout the remainder of the week the small, quiet trickle of God's presence became a raging flood of God's authority.

During my first week ever at a youth camp I saw visions, witnessed miracles, and experienced a dramatic life-altering shift that would change my future forever. The Holy Spirit became my lifelong companion. I would never be the same!

That first encounter with the Holy Spirit was amazing. I can remember it like it was yesterday, yet my supernatural experience would also need practical understanding if it was going to remain fresh. What a blessing It would have been to have a resource like this book during those first years of my spiritual journey. Instead, I was relegated to finding bits and pieces of information on the Holy Spirit wherever I could. My pastor rarely preached on the subject and youth meetings seemed more focused on fun than fire. Ultimately, I found resources to help my comprehension including tapes, books, sermons, Bible school lessons, and ministry friends. However, it took me years for my understanding to catch up with my experience in a way that I could teach others about the Holy Spirit. As I reflect on those days, I realize that one or two understandable, available resources would have equipped me with a stronger knowledge and made my witness much more effective.

New generations are hungry for the Holy Spirit, yet, in many instances, there is a void of spiritual knowledge and experience available to help guide them into God's fullness. At Oral Roberts University, I teach a class every year called Spirit-empowered Living. SEL (as we call it) is a required course so I have hundreds of young hearts and minds journeying with me on an exploration of the person and work of the Holy Spirit. During these classes each year, I discover that this generation is open, inquisitive, studious, and passionate about their relationship with God. They want to know more about the Holy Spirit and how He works. Teaching this class is one of my favorite duties as President. I love it. My constant prayer is that this generation will have life-altering encounters with the Holy Spirit that will revolutionize their walk with God as much as my sixteen-year-old baptism in the Spirit revolutionized me. And, that they will have a Biblical understanding of what happened to them making them strong and capable of teaching others.

*Empowered: Understanding the Holy Spirit in this Generation* written by Caleb Wehrli, is a practical resource to answer the need for clear information about the Holy Spirit in today's church. Caleb's wealth of spiritual experience informs each section of this volume and will help the reader apply practical application to Biblical concepts. Caleb will take you on a journey into understanding what the Spirit does and how He works in today's world.

Whether you are a pastor or a parishioner you will benefit from this work. Your hunger for the Holy Spirit will increase. Your understanding of Biblical teaching about the fruit, gifts, and work of the Holy Spirit will grow. And, you will be inspired to live a Spirit-empowered life in the 21st century. New generations especially will find this resource helpful in bringing definition to what the Spirit is doing in their heart and life. I would encourage you to take some moments in prayer after each chapter and ask God to allow these principles of His word to come alive in you.

My baptism in the Holy Spirit 45+ years ago changed my life forever. I would simply not have survived spiritually without a daily infusion of God's presence. I can tell you emphatically that knowing the Holy Spirit in a personal way has made all the difference. He has led me through numerous life decisions, helped me raise two great children, instructed me in my marriage to the best woman on earth, inspired me to dream big dreams, used me to win the lost, empowered me to see and do the miraculous, covered me in times of spiritual warfare, spoke to me in moments of personal despair and comforted me through it all. I simply could not and would not want to live without His constant companionship. My prayer is that you will experience this same miraculous power and that years from now you will look back on this moment to realize this book made a profound difference in your relationship with God. New generations are spiritually hungry and *Empowered: Understanding the Holy Spirit in this Generation* is going to make a tangible difference!

—Dr. William M. Wilson
Empowered21 Global Chair
Oral Roberts University President
Pentecostal World Fellowship Chair

# introduction

**D**o we really understand the Holy Spirit? Have we experienced His fullness in our generation? As I reflect on questions such as these, my heart burns for this generation to have a fresh encounter with the presence and power of the Holy Spirit like I did in my late teens and early twenties. These encounters transformed the trajectory of my life and ultimately led me towards a commitment to share Jesus and His power everywhere I go. Over the past twenty years, I have had the unique privilege of traveling to over sixty-five countries around the globe. I have visited churches from Asia to Africa, America to Israel, and everywhere in between.

My answer to whether we understand and have experienced the Holy Spirit is simply this—many in the global body of Christ simply aren't living in the fullness of what Jesus died for. For some, the Holy Spirit is an unwanted source of controversy. To others, He is a formula to be utilized for personal aggrandizement. At least some say He is an 'it'; others call Him a force.

The point is that as the church expands globally, the need to operate in the fullness of the Spirit's power becomes increasingly essential. New territory in the kingdom will necessitate new cooperation with the Holy Spirit. This is especially true of the current generation God is raising up. They need an encounter with the third member of the Trinity in all of His power.

Over the past couple of decades, our emphasis in the global church has focused on the believers' authority and identities, presence-driven worship movements, outreach and creative evangelism, etc. All of these are essential for the work of Christ to move forward in our generation. Yet, without a deliberate return to the person of the Spirit, I fear that the next generation will miss the driving factor behind all such emphases.

During the past decade, we have witnessed an abundance of new church planting initiatives globally focusing on reaching the lost. For many, teaching about the Spirit presents uncertainties. Will new believers stick around if we talk about Him? How much more so if He actually shows up in power? Will the Spirit be a source of controversy? Or maybe even division?

This mindset of concern has caused many influential voices in the body of Christ to deliberately omit an emphasis on the Holy Spirit because of a lack of clarity or perceived abuses in generations before them. Could it be that these perceived abuses and excesses produced a swing in the opposite direction—away from the moving of the person of the Spirit? The end result is that there is a generation of upcoming leaders in the global church today in their teens, twenties, and early thirties who understand little of what it means to be Spirit-empowered.

This has created a global vacuum in the church. We have form and function, but we need a move of God's Spirit like never before. The Holy Spirit has been charged with the foundational role of building and sustaining the Church that Jesus said He would build. My desire is to see Him release another great awakening so that the entire world can experience the fullness of what Jesus paid for. In this book, I use personal stories, scriptural insight, and practical application to encourage each generation to experience and rely on the Holy Spirit on a regular basis. I am believing that He will release clear understanding and a fresh outpouring as we rediscover the power of the Holy Spirit in the twenty-first century. Are you ready?

# CHAPTER 1

# the spirit in the 21st century

O ur vehicle sped down a Cambodian highway. The past few days had been a whirlwind of ministry activity. We had preached at a conference for local pastors, distributed gifts at an orphanage that was recently started, and encouraged the local believers to remain resilient in the face of daunting challenges. Suddenly, my mind darted back to the road in front of us. A large crowd of people had congregated on the highway, slowing down traffic significantly. The scene in front of me was total pandemonium: some were shouting, others were crying, and fingers were pointed viciously.

I sensed the Holy Spirit telling us to stop.

"What is going on?" I asked our contact seated in the car with me.

"Who knows? We need to keep going as the crowd is agitated," he responded with concern in his voice.

"Can we stop and find out what happened?" I asked again.

"It's too dangerous for a foreigner," came his response.

Sensing my determination, our contact jumped out of the car with me, and we headed into the thick of the crowd. In the middle of the commotion, we saw a young thirteen or fourteen-year-old girl lying lifeless on the ground next to a mangled bicycle. We found out that moments earlier, she had been hit from behind by a semi-truck while riding her bike on a busy two-lane road. People around us screamed at one another with intensity, but no one was doing anything. The girl was most likely dead; she was bleeding, and she had no pulse. Suddenly, a memory flashed into my mind of a story I had read years ago about an English plumber named Smith Wigglesworth who became a preacher. In that moment, I recalled how he once prayed for a man who had suffered a heart attack and died right in front of him. Through the power of the Holy Spirit, the man had been immediately restored to life.

"We have to pray for the girl!" I declared loud enough to be heard by my contact over the accusations flying around us.

"What?" he asked in disbelief, unsure if he had heard me correctly.

We walked over to the girl and placed our hands on her asking the Holy Spirit to restore life into her body. Nothing happened. My contact looked at me with embarrassment etched on his face. I knew he wanted us to get out of there immediately.

"Let's pray one more time," I insisted.

This time as we laid hands on her head, the power of God filled her body. Suddenly, she gasped with a big breath and then sat upright as the crowd went silent.

## a defining moment

Every generation has a defining moment—an event that divides time and distinguishes between the before and after. Once the event takes place, nothing is the same. Our generation could talk about 9/11 or the outbreak of COVID-19 as such moments in history. Other people may talk about the Berlin Wall coming down or the assassination of John F. Kennedy. Following such events, the world changes—sometimes for the worse, sometimes for the better.

As Christ-followers, we celebrate a more impactful, era-defining moment than all the others combined. This annual celebration is known as Pentecost. It's when we remember what happened in the Upper Room with the arrival of the Holy Spirit to empower Jesus' disciples.

Acts chapter two depicts heaven infusing humanity with the power of God. Fire, wind, tongues, and thousands are swept into the kingdom after a single message mark this moment. People from all over the known world found Jesus that day. At least fifteen different nationalities experienced the explosive birth of the church that day. The era of the Spirit had arrived.

While Pentecost is clearly a very significant historical event, it's also a very powerful current event. In other words, Pentecost is not a monument to be commemorated; Pentecost is a movement still changing the world. The little girl on the side of the highway experienced the same power that was poured out on the Day of Pentecost. The Spirit is alive now! His goal is to make Jesus real to our generation. The question is simple. Will you be His hands and feet?

Many believers have been satisfied with reliving the past exploits of previous generations of Christ-followers. We talk about their adventures, honor their valiant obedience, and applaud their courage and conviction. Of course, there is nothing wrong with celebrating what God has done in the past . . . provided that we don't forget that the Holy Spirit is active today. Jesus is far more concerned with the movement of the church today than a monument to the past. The message given to the early church on the Day of Pentecost was that the Spirit wants to live through each of us to change our world. That message is not archaic or just a part of history; it is a message for today. We were designed to be Spirit-empowered!

## the twenty-first century

What I learned in Cambodia is that the Holy Spirit empowers us for any emergency. This girl needed a miracle, the Holy Spirit wanted to release it, and we were available for Him to use. It was a critical moment that required immediate attention. Can I remind us that our world has many such critical situations? The twenty-first century is full of spiritual emergencies. Lives are hanging in the balance in our generation. We are witnessing a global pandemic of drug addiction, suicide, sexual perversion, and identity confusion.

The result is that we are part of one of the most broken and confused generations ever to live. We must get the message of God's hope and power out to them. This is where the Holy Spirit comes in. Our unique moment in world history demands people who understand the Spirit's supernatural operation. Learning how to partner with the Holy Spirit is essential to becoming a twenty-first century Christian.

Great advances in technology, communication, and scientific discovery have marked the twenty-first century. To keep pace with the rapid changes in our world, the church has introduced new worship styles, developed fresh outreach plans, integrated technology, and emphasized reaching the lost through new church plants. We are rediscovering more and more about Jesus and His love for people. Sadly, these advances can sometimes create a sense of superiority among us. We think that we have accomplished much in our own strength and ability. We must always remember that the primary power source of the church is the Holy Spirit!

What our hurting world desperately needs in this hour is Jesus! The only way they will see Him is through you and me. Representing Jesus is never easy. We won't be able to accomplish this with human resources, no matter how brilliant we may be. We must have the Holy Spirit to help us with this colossal task. I like how Oral Roberts used to say, "It's the job of the Holy Spirit to bring back to earth the full, unlimited power of Jesus."

## the unlimited power of Jesus

Imagine with me the full, unlimited power of Jesus being free to operate in our world. How many people would be healed? Who would be set free from demonic oppression? Which cities and nations would see revival? What solutions would be released for ending poverty or eradicating racism? Remember, we are talking about the unlimited power of Jesus—the kind of power that restores dead girls on Cambodian highways to life. Now imagine what would happen in your life. What bondages would be broken in you? What kind of ministry or business steps would you implement? How would you share your testimony? Who would you share the message with if you were certain of Christ's unlimited power?

Do you see how important it is that we embrace the message of what the Holy Spirit started at Pentecost? The Holy Spirit gives us everything we need to make Jesus alive and real in our generation. He fills us and clothes us with Jesus. In a very real sense, we continue Christ's ministry in the here and now. Jesus is seen and revealed through us as we experience the fullness of the Spirit.

The global youth culture has become saturated with the paranormal and the superhuman experience. The Marvel movies have witnessed a resurgence of the superheroes: Superman, Batman, Antman, the Hulk, and Thor, just to name a few. In addition, we have seen paranormal activity and outright witchcraft normalized in this generation through numerous popular novel series and along many other similar storylines. What does this fascination with the transcendent tell us? The bottom line is that this generation is craving something beyond itself. Our generation is craving a spiritual experience.

This inner longing will be filled with something. My desire is that this God-given hunger be met by the supernatural power of the Holy Spirit! Jesus promised rivers of living water would satisfy the deep, inner longing of the human soul (John 7:38). And just in case there is any question about the meaning of His statement, John specified in the next verse: "By this He meant the Spirit" (7:39, NIV). Only the supernatural overflow of the Holy Spirit can satisfy this hunger!

You are Jesus' hands and feet in the twenty-first century. The church is not the four walls of a building; the church is you and I walking in unity to see Jesus glorified. In order for this to happen, our lives—talents, time, and treasure—must be infused by the

Holy Spirit. Only then can we demonstrate Jesus to our broken and hurting world. In the twenty-first century, it is precisely this dimension of spiritual power that will open doors for the message of Christ in previously untouched spheres of influence. Like never before, a manifestation of the Spirit's power is our most precious commodity.

This book is all about learning how to make that happen. We are going to talk about some of the most important concepts related to understanding the Holy Spirit:

- **His identity:** The Holy Spirit is a person.
- **Being led by the Spirit:** The Holy Spirit wants to lead us in everything.
- **Receiving the Spirit:** The Holy Spirit wants to give you God's power.
- **Understanding the Spirit's purpose:** The Holy Spirit is on a mission.
- **Partnering with the Spirit:** The Holy Spirit wants to express His gifts through you.

As you read this book, my prayer is that you will receive a fresh infusion of the Spirit's power to demonstrate Jesus to our lost and hurting generation.

CHAPTER 2

# the arrival of the holy spirit

**T**he Holy Spirit shows up where He is invited, and when He shows up, things always change. While we don't know exactly what His arrival was like two thousand years ago on the Day of Pentecost, we do know what happens when He shows up today. I remember being in Sierra Leone, West Africa, as a twenty-three year old, about to preach in the National Soccer Stadium to over eighty thousand people. I was scared to stand in front of so many people and share the gospel. My father-in-law was supposed to be preaching that night, but he had also been invited to share in another city on that evening, so he asked me to preach in his place. He told me, "You've seen me do it before, and now it's your turn!" As I stood on the platform, my mind raced: *What will I say? Will the people listen to a young preacher?*

Finally, I prayed a simple prayer and asked the Holy Spirit to show up and do what only He could do. A peace swept over me as I started to preach. His presence intensified over the course of the next hour. He showed up in an amazing way that evening as thousands of people responded to receive Christ, and scores were healed almost immediately as they prayed. It was such an incredible evening. His arrival literally transformed the atmosphere of that stadium setting many people free! We know that His arrival two thousand years ago changed things in Jerusalem instantly, and He continues to change things today wherever He's invited to show up—both in West Africa as well as the place where you are reading this book.

How do we know that the power of the Holy Spirit is available to do the greater works of the Father? Is this just hyperbole or exaggerated exegesis of the text? Or is the Spirit really still present in our generation? In order to answer this question, we need to look at the operation of the Spirit in the Old Testament. We could look at multiple examples where He anointed various people for specific tasks. The idea of anointing implied that someone was set apart for a specific purpose and clothed with the power necessary to accomplish it. Interestingly, once the task was completed, the Spirit's presence would lift, and He would return to heaven. In other words, the anointing didn't last because the empowerment was temporary.

This changed with the ministry of Jesus. In the third chapter of Luke, Jesus went to the Jordan River to be baptized by His cousin, John. As He descended into the water, the Spirit of God fell upon Him, similar to Old Testament occurrences. Luke states, "Now when all the people were baptized, and when Jesus also had been baptized and was praying, the heavens were opened, and the Holy Spirit descended on him in bodily form, like a dove" (3:21-22, ESV). Until now, this event had following the normal pattern of the Holy Spirit's interactions on the face of the earth. What followed isn't so much what the text says as much as what it doesn't say. At no point did the Spirit ever alight and return to heaven. In other words, the Spirit became the present and active empowerment in the life and ministry of Jesus.

No wonder Jesus could stand up in the synagogue in Nazareth and read from the scroll of Isaiah, the prophet. "The Spirit of the Lord is upon me, because He has anointed me to proclaim good news to the poor, He has sent me to proclaim liberty to the captives and recovering of sight to the blind, to set at liberty those who are oppressed" (Luke 4:18, ESV). Do you see the importance of that statement? Jesus was saying that the Spirit had come and would remain upon Him to accomplish His ministry.

In fact, that was how John the Baptist recognized Jesus. "I myself did not know him, but he who sent me to baptize with water said to me, 'He on whom you see the Spirit descend and remain, this is he who baptizes with the Holy Spirit'" (John 1:33, ESV). Many years later, Peter would summarize the gospel for the gentiles at Cornelius's house by explaining "how God anointed Jesus of Nazareth with the Holy Spirit and with power. He went about doing good and healing all who were oppressed by the devil, for God was with him" (Act 10:38, ESV).

The point is simply this: If Jesus needed the empowerment of the Holy Spirit in order to do ministry, how much more do you and I? Please understand that Jesus' dependency on the Spirit wasn't weakness or insufficiency. Instead, Jesus exemplified Spirit-empowered ministry for His disciples. No wonder we see multiple times throughout the gospels where Jesus promised that He would send the Holy Spirit to remain with His disciples and to empower them for ministry. One clear example is found in Luke 24:49, where Jesus instructed the disciples to stay in Jerusalem until they were clothed with power from on high. This came as no surprise to them because He had already set the example for what He expected His followers to implement— Spirit-empowered life and ministry.

## the day of pentecost

The Holy Spirit's arrival to empower the disciples to continue Christ's life and ministry occurs in Acts chapter 2. We refer to this event as the Day of Pentecost. Many Christians in our generation have a negative impression due to stereotypes about the word Pentecost. This is tragic because the word has no negative connotation to it. Pentecost is derived from the Greek word meaning fifty or fiftieth because it occurs fifty days after the feast of Passover. The Jewish celebration of Pentecost is also often called the Feast of Harvest or First Fruits because it is when the Jewish people celebrated the annual harvest of their crops.

Can you see that it is no coincidence that Jesus died on the Passover and chose to send the Holy Spirit to His disciples on the Day of Pentecost? Jesus knows what He is doing. The message is that His resurrection must be shared with others. This is why He sent the Holy Spirit to empower the disciples to continue His ministry after Him. He is gathering a spiritual harvest from every nation. Hopefully, you can see that the term Pentecost has no negative biblical connotation to it.

From Pentecost, we derive the term Pentecostal. In its simplest definition, the word refers to people who believe that the same power of the Holy Spirit that Jesus released on the Day of Pentecost is still available for believers today. Amazingly, many Christian statisticians estimate that there are over 650 million Pentecostals or Holy Spirit-empowered believers globally. It is considered to be the fastest-growing part of the Christian church in our generation. Literally, Pentecostals can be found in every corner of our world in the twenty-first century.

Where does the controversy regarding the term Pentecost arise? The answer is in the interpretation and practice of some people within the Pentecostal movement. Unfortunately, there have been excesses and abuses in certain contexts. People have emphasized strange manifestations and other practices that aren't even in the Bible. This has created hesitation on the part of some believers today to embrace the idea of Pentecost. Please remember, however, that this doesn't discredit the idea of Pentecost in Acts 2.

Often when I travel in Asia, I am offered knock-off accessories. For example, one time, I was offered a $50 iPhone that didn't even last more than a few weeks. What would you think if someone offered to buy me a real iPhone, and I refused because of negative experiences in my past with a fake version? You would probably say, "Caleb, this isn't *that*. Don't miss a blessing because of a bad past experience." In the same way, my appeal to you is simple. Don't miss out on the fullness of Jesus' promised blessing in your life because of a previous negative impression of the Holy Spirit. When you hear the term Pentecost or Pentecostal, think Spirit-empowered Acts 2—the Holy Spirit's EMPOWERMENT of Christ-followers, and the idea of harvest and ongoing power for your life and ministry—today.

## harvest

Before we close this chapter, it's important to develop this idea of harvest one step further. Most Christians see the event of Pentecost as the birth of the early church. The outpouring of the Spirit empowering the 120 to go and be Jesus' hands and feet all over the world. Scripture tells us that there were people gathered "from every nation under heaven" in the city that day (Acts 2:5, NIV). The Feast of Pentecost attracted people from all over the ancient world. Startled, these people heard the disciples speaking in their local languages following the Holy Spirit's empowerment. At least fourteen different people groups and geographical locations outside of Jerusalem are mentioned. "Amazed and perplexed," they heard God's wonders communicated to them in their own languages, and "they asked one another, 'What does this mean?'" (Acts 2:12, NIV).

Peter stood up and delivered one of the fieriest messages recorded in Scripture. Three thousand people were convicted and surrendered their lives to Jesus. This implies that, during the first invitation in the church's history, people from multiple nations and ethnic backgrounds responded to the glorious message of Jesus' grace. This is consistent with Jesus' promise in Acts 1:8 (NIV) just days prior to the Holy Spirit's arrival, "But you will receive power when the Holy Spirit has come upon you, and you will be my witnesses in Jerusalem and in all Judea and Samaria, and to the end of the earth."

Notice the geographical dimensions in this verse encompassing a multi-ethnic expansion of the gospel. Is it any wonder that, from a small group of 120 believers, Jesus' church has literally spread to every corner of planet Earth? The message of the Holy Spirit coming on the Day of Pentecost is unmistakable: Jesus desires to empower His church for a global harvest. We, in our generation, are in the middle of one of the greatest fulfillments of that message. What an awesome time to be alive!

Why do we need the empowerment of the Holy Spirit? The simple answer is two-fold: First, Jesus needed it, and secondly, the gospel message is for all people groups. Do we really believe that if Jesus were alive on the face of the earth in the twenty-first century that He would attempt to do ministry without the empowerment of the Holy Spirit? Are the challenges that the world faces any less daunting than when He ministered in the first century? Of course not! We must do ministry the same way that Jesus did—under the influence of the Holy Spirit. Only then will we experience the same power and authority that accompanied Jesus' life and ministry.

Secondly, every nation, every tribe, and every tongue must hear the good news. Why is this so important? I believe it's because Jesus made global evangelism a sign of His Second Coming. "And this gospel of the kingdom will be preached as a witness to all nations and then the end will come" (Matthew 24:14, NIV). When will Jesus come back? This verse seems to imply that it's not going to happen until the gospel of the kingdom is proclaimed throughout our world. The Holy Spirit wants to empower us to share this glorious message.

The generation we live in is in desperate need of Christ's power and grace. Jesus wants to fill you with the power of His Spirit so that you can partner with Him to bring in the greatest harvest of souls that our world has ever known.

CHAPTER 3

# the purpose of the holy spirit

**W**e were in Ecuador on one of my first trips to South America, leading a team of young people. Our ministry focused on sharing Jesus in the streets and plazas and praying for people to get healed. One afternoon we were in a park ministering to about fifteen people. Our team was about to lead several people in the prayer of salvation. Unexpectedly, a lady came walking up with two small children. She had missed almost the entirety of our presentation. Without missing a beat, she said she was ready to give her life to Jesus and wanted to receive special prayer.

I was ministering to her through a translator.

She asked me the question: "Why are you really here?"

I didn't understand what she meant, so I asked the translator if I had missed something. Nope.

She asked the exact same question again: "Why are you really here?"

I didn't know what to say, so I remained silent.

With tears in her eyes, she looked at me and said, "You are here because of me."

She then proceeded to share her story. Her husband had left her a note that very morning that he was leaving her and the children.

In a moment of sheer desperation, she felt totally over-whelmed and cried out to God, *If you are real, then I need you to show me yourself today.* She decided to go on a walk in the park near her apartment. As she approached, she could hear us preaching, and she immediately knew that the message was for her.

Why do we do what we do? People are hurting, broken, devastated. The Holy Spirit's power is poured out in our lives to help us be witnesses. We are able to share Jesus' love in a way that people can experience Him for themselves. He uses even the seemingly most obscure events and moments of life to draw people to the Son. The purpose of the Holy Spirit is to fulfill the plan of God. The plan of God is to reach and redeem people, and He does that by using us to be His witnesses.

The outpouring of the Spirit is directly connected to God's heart for other people. The Holy Spirit wants people everywhere to know Jesus as their Lord and Savior. Jesus told His disciples that they were going to receive the Spirit's power to be His witnesses (Acts 1:8). On the Day of Pentecost, at least three thousand people made personal decisions to surrender their lives through Peter's preaching. Luke tells us that they were pierced to the heart as they listened to Peter's first message after his baptism in the Spirit (Acts 2:37). We see, from this event, the purpose of the baptism of the Spirit—to equip Christ's followers to be greater witnesses and fulfill the Great Commission (Matthew 28:18). Nothing has changed; the purpose of the Spirit is to make believers bold witnesses for Christ!

Do you think someone's final words carry weight? A person's parting instructions or exhortations have extreme significance. They are often the most important words that a person can leave behind. Matthew 28 offers us a glimpse into Christ's final words to His disciples. His focus is on making disciples globally. Immediately, we recognize that Jesus is thinking much bigger than Jerusalem; He has a passion for the world. This is why this passage is referred to as the Great Commission—or, as I like to say, Christ's mandate. I firmly believe that His last words should be our first priority.

The interesting thing about Christ's mandate is that He is sharing it with His disciples. In other words, He is including others in His global plan. Their participation, in fact, is essential to making the mandate a reality. Jesus tells them that, from that point forward, their mission must be His global mandate. This is why it's called the Great Commission. A commission is a mission that requires both partnership and commitment from multiple parties.

Christ's final words go beyond the first generation of disciples to every believer in every generation. In the kingdom of God, everyone has a part to play. Interestingly, Jesus gave the same mandate to all of His disciples despite their different backgrounds and abilities. It was a corporate mandate to be His witnesses. In effect, He was saying, "Come partner with me on this great mission to change the world." This is also the mandate and mission that Jesus has given to our generation in the twenty-first century.

Did you know that as a follower of Jesus, you have the potential to change the world? Actually, it's more than just potential. You now have a responsibility to partner with Him to change the world. Change the world? Does the idea of a global mission seem too big? If we make disciples of all nations, we will change the world! For this to happen, we must reach people with the love of Christ. People are part of families. Families form the social fabric of any society. Societies dictate the direction of nations. Therefore, Jesus is all about changing the nations!

A young man surrendered his heart to Jesus in the middle of Africa. He was a witch doctor consulting demons and placing spells on people. Once he came to Christ, his family was impacted, and soon they accepted Jesus also. The young man decided to study in a Bible school and became a pastor. Many people in his town heard the gospel through his ministry. Thousands of people have been impacted by his life. How did this happen? A new believer from a distant church knocked on his door one morning. The witch doctor had been harassed the night before by the evil spirits that he thought he controlled. The young believer wanted to share the love of Jesus with him, and his ordeal had prepared him to listen! Jesus' love touched his heart, and he surrendered his life on the spot. The gospel still changes the world!

## empowered for mission

Let's be honest. Christ's mandate can seem a bit daunting, right? Current statistics tell us that the global population is somewhere around 7.8 billion people. According to the Joshua Project, 3.23 billion people are still considered totally unreached. Of the 17,425 different ethnic groups in our world, some 7,400 are still unreached. The world is a big place; the world is a lost place. As such, making disciples of the nations (ethnic groups) can feel overwhelming. I know it does for me.

Being a bold witness for Christ requires a power source outside of my personal ability or capacity.

This is exactly what Jesus promised the disciples in Acts 1:8—they would receive a power from on high that would enable them to be His witnesses globally: Jerusalem, Judea, Samaria, and to the ends of the world. In other words, Jesus was saying, "I know this Great Commission idea sounds rather intimidating, and you feel inadequate, but you need to understand. For that reason, I am sending the Spirit."

The purpose of the Holy Spirit is to give us the boldness, courage, and conviction necessary to be witnesses to change the world. Some people think that this could never happen in their lives. They think that changing the world might be for "pastors" or "ministers," but they see no way for their lives to be included in this global mandate. That is simply not true. When Peter stood up to explain the Spirit's outpouring in Acts 2, he based his message on the book of Joel. He said, "And it will come to pass afterward that I will pour out my Spirit on all flesh" (Joel 2:28-29, NIV). Notice that the Spirit isn't reserved for a few select super-spiritual Jewish people who were close to Jesus. Rather, Peter says that everyone is a candidate for the power of the Holy Spirit.

Perhaps you feel like your life is too messed up or that you have made too many mistakes to experience the Spirit's world-changing power. Keep in mind that Peter was so insecure that he couldn't even stand up for Jesus to some household servants (Matthew 28). In fact, he literally called curses down on himself when someone identified him as a disciple. Talk about betrayal and fear. Yet, forty or so days later, he preached so boldly on the streets of Jerusalem that thousands of people were moved to repentance. How can this kind of transformation take place? The only explanation is that he had a personal encounter with the power of the Holy Spirit. If Jesus can do it for Peter, He can do it for you too!

## seven mountains

When we talk about being global witnesses, it can be difficult to know what this means for us personally. Are we saying that every believer has to be a preacher? Or that each Christian needs to be in full-time ministry? Or that we all have to move to distant lands? If I move to Brazil, does that mean that my Brazilian friends have to move to the United States? Or Africa? Or China? In order to answer these questions, we need to understand that society is made up of seven mountains or spheres of influence. These seven spheres hold up every society around the world. If the gospel of Christ is going to produce long-term change in the world, then Jesus' followers need to influence these seven areas in society.

The seven areas are as follows: church, government, media arts and entertainment, education, business, science and technology, and family. Placed together, these seven areas provide the framework by which our societies function. Remove one area, and the fabric of society starts to unravel. My point is that if we are going to change the world, then we have to change these seven areas of society. If we are going to make disciples of all the nations per Jesus' decree, then we must disciple people within these seven building blocks of society. The

Greek word for nations is *ethnos,* which means people groups. We have been given a mandate to change the people groups of this world, and the only way this can happen is by changing the societies where these people groups exist. This is why the power of the Holy Spirit gives you boldness and creativity—to change your world.

Let's go back to the question of how to be a global witness for Christ. Where is your world? I can guarantee that your world falls within at least one of these seven arenas of societal influence. Whether you are a banker, schoolteacher, electrician, engineer, policeman, or construction worker, your vocation is the platform that the Holy Spirit uses to make you a witness for Christ. Could Jesus call you to move to another country and be His witness there? Sure. However, if we aren't faithful and diligent to transform the parts of the world in which we live, it will be difficult to do so in a cross-cultural context. The Holy Spirit empowers us to start right where we are.

## start where you are

How do we start being Christ's witnesses in our current contexts? I think that answer lies in two areas. The Holy Spirit empowers us both internally to walk out God's will and externally to share Christ with boldness. Both are vital to being a vibrant witness for Jesus. Let's talk about the internal component of the Spirit's work first. This is power to walk out the will of God for your life.

Have you ever met someone who talks a big talk with lots of extraordinary claims and assertions, but his or her lifestyle doesn't match what is being said? We sometimes call this hypocrisy. The

Greek word is *hypokrites*. The meaning is connected to a stage actor. Often an actor would put on an elaborate mask and costume to play a certain character or role. Once the show was over, the person took off the mask and stopped pretending to be someone else. Reasonably, many Christians feel like stage actors sharing a message externally that they don't live internally. Imagine sharing Christ's freedom with someone who knows that you are actually a slave to sin in an area of your life. It will be difficult to convince that person that he or she needs Christ's freedom because your message is contrary to your example.

The good news is that the Holy Spirit gives us the strength and power we need to live consistently with God's will so that our witness is credible to the world around us. People are drawn to us because they can see something different. They see that God's power is operating deep inside our hearts to produce lasting transformation within us. This gives our witness authority and compassion because we are sharing the freedom we have experienced from a place of tenderness because we know our own struggles.

The second idea is that of external power to share. Here are some questions that will help illustrate what this concept looks like in practice. What has Jesus done for you? Has He forgiven your sins? Did He give you freedom from a particular bondage or addiction? Tell other people in your sphere of influence what Jesus did for you. While people may be able to debate your theology, they can't argue with your personal testimony. We also need to show people what Jesus has done for us. This often looks like practical acts of service. This can include feeding the hungry, doing errands for a neighbor, taking care of widows and orphans, etc. When we share what God has done for us through practical actions, we are illustrating God's love for people. Sharing and showing are two ways the Spirit empowers you to change your world—one person at a time.

Several years ago, I was ministering in China. After the services, I went to dinner with a prominent businessman. He shared with me how the Spirit was opening doors for him and his friends to share Jesus all over China. The government restricts the organized church in China, but he said that the regular working people were changing the nation. They were doing this by sharing, within their particular spheres of influence, what Jesus had done inside of them. The internal and external power of the Spirit provides the boldness these regular believers need to change the nation! Did you know that there are an estimated one hundred million Christians in China today because of faithful Spirit-empowered witnesses committed to showing and sharing the love of Jesus?

As we close this chapter, may I challenge you to think about your world? I mean the place of your influence. Jesus has called you to accept His mandate. This is your mission field! The Holy Spirit will give you the power you need to share His love with the people around you in practical ways. They will see the validity of your witness for Christ through the overflow of His power in your life. For the Holy Spirit, the supernatural is always natural. His supernatural power makes an impact in our world naturally as we show His love and share what Jesus has done for us. This is the supernatural expressed in the natural. This is how we change the world!

CHAPTER 4

# the person of the holy spirit

The Holy Spirit has the answer to every question we face in life. He has the insight and capacity to lead us because He is a person. As a person, He communicates God's perfect purpose and will for our lives so that we don't have to guess what we should do. As a young Christian, I remember trying to understand this concept. When I finally surrendered my life completely to Christ, I finally understood the idea of His personhood. I heard some people talking about the Holy Spirit being their friend and speaking to them. Then I started being intentional to have conversations with Him. This is only possible when we recognize that as a person and a friend, He has a voice and desires to communicate with us. As I became intentional to listen for His voice, I started to recognize that He was speaking to me with specific guidance and direction for my life.

The direct result of my communion with Him as a person has been a growing sensitivity to His voice. What I have learned is that it is important to speak to Him as any other person. What do I mean? Communication is a process of not just speaking but also of listening. When we stop and listen for His still small voice speaking on the inside, we receive great insight. This is why the daily discipline of prayer is so important. It involves both speaking and listening so that we can respond with appropriate action steps. We must always remember that He is a person who desires to communicate with us.

## questions

Asking questions is vital in discovering the truth about something. Who is the Holy Spirit? How can we know Him? Sadly, there is much confusion in the body of Christ concerning the identity of the Holy Spirit. Is He a force? A specialized power? Some see the Spirit as an inanimate force that can be controlled and manipulated for personal interests. This is a total misunderstanding of what Scripture tells us. Throughout God's Word, we see that He is a person with emotions, a will, and a mind. Jesus said that the Holy Spirit would serve as His replacement on the earth (John 14:16-26, 15:26, and 16:7).

The Spirit establishes and represents the lordship of Christ in our lives. C. H. Spurgeon once remarked that, "It is the job of the Holy Spirit to produce the personhood of Jesus." Only a person can represent another person. With all this talk about personhood, it's important to discuss the Trinity.

## the trinity

The term Trinity has to do with the idea of three. It is the idea that God expresses Himself in three personalities throughout Scripture. These are God the Father, God the Son, and God the Holy Spirit. We speak of the Holy Spirit as being the third member of the Trinity. John 14:16 (NASB) is a great illustration of this idea: "I will ask the Father, and *he* will give you another Helper, that he may be with you forever." Notice Jesus doesn't call the Spirit an 'it' or a "force." Other verses that describe this idea are found in Luke 1:35, 2 Corinthians 13:14, and Matthew 28:19. In other words, God is one God in the form of three coeternal persons of the same essence. This can be a difficult concept to grasp.

A Muslim confronted a Christian and accused him of being an idolater because he worshipped three gods.

The Christ-follower responded with a question: "Are you married to your wife?"

The man replied: "Yes."

He asked the Muslim another question: "Are you a father?"

Again the man replied in the affirmative.

He asked a third question, "Do you have a father?"

The man went strangely quiet, for he recognized that he was a husband, father, and son all at the same time. While this analogy is limited when applied to the concept of the Trinity, it at least offers us a glimpse into God's nature—three in one. The Holy Spirit is one of the members of the Trinity and as such, is fully God.

Genesis 1:26 (NIV) records the creation account with the statement: "Let us make man in our image, in our likeness." Do you see God speaking of Himself in the plural? This is the idea of the Trinity. The Father, the Son, and the Holy Spirit are together at the beginning of the world. They partner in the creation process and will continue in the same unity for the rest of eternity. We often talk about the Holy Spirit with the definite article "the." As a person, this doesn't make sense.

Would you say to me, "Hello, the Caleb Wehrli. How are you today?" Or do we pray to "the Jesus" or refer to our Heavenly Father as "the Father"? Can you imagine someone praying, "Dear the Father, I thank you for sending your Son, the Jesus, to live in the Caleb's heart"? While this may just seem like a grammatical issue, it has a theological dimension to it. If we are really to see the Holy Spirit as a person, it often helps believers to drop the definitive article and call Him by His actual name: Holy Spirit. In this way, we are personalizing our interaction with Him, so we can develop a relationship with Him.

## surrender

My point is to establish the personhood and importance of yielding and surrendering to the Spirit. Many Christians have received Jesus as their Savior, but they haven't positioned Him as their Lord. This is an important distinction. Who doesn't like the benefits of forgiveness, peace, blessings, and eternal life that come through salvation? By contrast, the demands of lordship require some actions from us: obedience, consecration, and surrender to name just a few. Embracing His lordship is more challenging, but vitally important for our everyday life.

Why is any of this important? I thought we were talking about the Holy Spirit? Since the idea of lordship is demonstrated in our surrender to Christ, in a similar way we are to yield our spirit to the Holy Spirit, so He can occupy His rightful place in our lives. Our surrender to Jesus as Lord, allows us to be in a position where we can be fully surrendered to the Holy Spirit in our life.

In other words, if Jesus isn't really Lord of your life, then a person cannot be surrendered to the Holy Spirit. In so doing we will have denied one of the most important aspects of the Spirit's personhood—His direction and leadership in our lives. This dispels the myth of Him being a force, or a power or an 'it' that we can control for our benefit. When we surrender to the Spirit, we are welcoming His leadership and direction in our lives. This involves active participation on our end.

The other important aspect of the Spirit's personhood is that of interaction. He deals with us as people and expects us to respond in kind. Many people make the claim that the demonstration of the Spirit's power is based exclusively on God's sovereignty. It goes something like this: "If the Spirit wants to do something supernatural, then He can do something supernatural." This makes the Spirit into an unknowable force instead of a person because it takes any responsibility off us to know Him as a person. We become passive agents because we start to believe that our interactions with Him have very little to do with the demonstration of His power.

I see many problems with such an approach. It reminds me of the church elder who looked at young William Carey burning with a call to the take gospel to the unreached of India and told him, "Young man, sit down; when God is pleased to convert the heathen world, He will do it without your help or mine." Thankfully, Carey paid no attention to such a warped view of God's sovereignty. He refused to be passive and unmoved, instead choosing personal participation in world missions. Likewise, the Spirit desires to move in our generation, but He does so within the context of people who have surrendered to His will and know Him personally. Lordship implies responsive action on our end, obedience.

## the role of the holy spirit

As a person, the Holy Spirit has a very clear and defined role that He desires to play in our lives. What does this role look like?

Jesus begins to answer this question for His disciples in John 14:16 when He says: "*And I will pray to the Father, and he shall give you another Comforter, that he may abide with you forever.*" Have you ever gone through a really difficult time?

I can still remember the devastating reality when my Father-in-law, Pastor Billy Joe Daugherty, the founding pastor of Victory Church in Tulsa, Oklahoma, passed away from cancer at the age of fifty-seven. It was a difficult time for friends and church members, but it was especially challenging for all of the members of his immediate family. Despite the great sorrow we felt as we grieved the loss of this great man, there was an unusual sense of comfort and peace that enveloped each family member in the days and months following his departure. What was that? This was the presence of the Holy Spirit. He provided the desperate comfort that the family needed in that moment and on numerous days since that time.

Jesus provides more insight into the role of the Holy Spirit. He tells us in John 16:8 (NIV) that "When he (the Holy Spirit) comes, he will prove the world to be in the wrong about sin and righteousness and judgment." Sometimes we get uncomfortable when we talk about conviction. This is unfortunate because conviction is important for our spiritual health. It is similar to going to the doctor for an appointment.

If you had a serious illness like cancer and the doctor said to you, "Everything looks fine to me," how would you respond? Most likely, you would be upset that the doctor didn't take your condition very seriously. A painkiller simply doesn't work with life-threatening issues. The role of the doctor is to help you get better, not pretend there isn't an issue. In the same way, Jesus promises that the Holy Spirit convicts us of sin. The reason He does this isn't that He doesn't like us, but rather it's because He wants to make us whole. The conviction of the Spirit in your life is vital. Responding to His gentle prodding will produce spiritual vitality in your life.

We have talked about conviction and comfort. This is so important because His conviction makes us want to be more like Jesus. This is, in fact, the primary goal of His work in our lives. Holy Spirit helps us become more like Christ.

Let's read 2 Corinthians 3:17-18 from the New Living Translation. "*For the Lord is the Spirit, and wherever the Spirit of the Lord is, there is freedom. So all of us who have had that veil removed can see and reflect the glory of the Lord. And the Lord—who is the Spirit—makes us more and more like him as we are changed into his glorious image.*" What an awesome thought; we are called to be more like Jesus. What would your life look like if you were more like Jesus? Would you be more patient? More kind? More joyful?

The good news is that Jesus sent the Holy Spirit to help you become more like Jesus! He wants to empower you to be more like Christ. Being Christ-like includes both Christ's character as well as Christ's power. Christ-like character is described in Galatians 5:22-23 as being fruit that is produced by the presence of the Spirit in the life of a believer. "*But the fruit of the Spirit is love, joy, peace, patience, kindness, goodness, faithfulness, gentleness and self-control.*" The Spirit is always moving inside of us to produce the fruit of Christ-like character.

Christ-like power is explained in Acts 1;8, where Jesus says, "But you will receive power when the Holy Spirit comes on you; and you will be my witnesses in Jerusalem, and in all Judea and Samaria, and to the ends of the earth." The Spirit empowers us to be witnesses for Christ.

I remember being in Ecuador sharing the gospel. There was a man with a broken hand who didn't know Jesus. I knew the Holy Spirit had empowered me to be a witness for Jesus. And I knew Jesus wanted this man to experience His love. So I prayed for his hand, and instantly Jesus healed his hand. The miracle confirmed the message; I was a witness of Christ by the Spirit's power.

Do you remember what Jesus said in John 14:12 (NKJV)? He made an incredible statement: "He who believes in me, the works that I do he will do also, and greater works than these he will do, because I go to the Father." How can this be? It seems too good to be true. The answer is that the power of the Holy Spirit is available in your life to do the greater works of the Father.

# CHAPTER 5

# the personality of the holy spirit

**W**e have already talked about God the Holy Spirit being a member of the Trinity as a unique person and how important it is for us to develop a personal relationship with Him. He is not an "it" or a "force" or a "power." He is a person with real personal attributes that allow us to know Him intimately. Interestingly, according to a recent survey, sixty-one percent of protestant Christians hold to a view that the Holy Spirit is not a person or a living entity, but a symbol of God's presence. This is tragic because adopting such a perspective will destroy a person's desire to know Him intimately.

I can still remember the feelings of intimidation and fear when I first started preaching in the mid-1990s in rural villages and small churches during mission trips with my local church. Initially, I thought the responsibility was up to me to make sure I had a good Word for the people, but it didn't take long for me to realize that it was a disaster waiting to happen. I couldn't save anyone, heal anyone, or set anyone free! These are works that only the Holy Spirit can accomplish, but that doesn't mean that I have no part to play. My role is to be in fellowship with Him, know Him, and allow Him to work through me.

This reality of the Holy Spirit changed the way I looked at the Christian life because I stopped seeing myself down here and God up there, and I started to see the Holy Spirit with me wherever I go. This perspective has transformed my life and ministry.

Since the Holy Spirit is actively with us, our calling is to get to know His personality and desires so that we can yield to His plans. Think of that for a moment—the Holy Spirit has a specific desire for your life and future. He is not a silent partner in your salvation experience with God, but He is an active participant in the process of God fulfilling His will on the earth through you!

Now every time I have an opportunity to speak or encourage people, I always pray a simple prayer of invitation quietly to God as a sign of surrender to the personality and desires of the Holy Spirit. My prayer goes something like this, *Holy Spirit . . . have your way . . . do what You want to do in this place . . . You are welcome here . . . and I ask You to show me what You want to do . . . I trust YOU . . . I rely on YOU . . . I cannot do this without YOU! Have YOUR way today through me!* I believe understanding the personality of the Holy Spirit is one of the greatest things that we can realize as Christians. It helps us walk in sync with the Father's will for our lives, and it allows us to be used by God here on the earth.

Jesus discusses the personality of the Holy Spirit with His disciples in John 14:16-17 (HCSB). "And I will ask the Father, and He will give you *another Counselor* to be with you forever—He is the Spirit of truth. The world is unable to receive Him because it doesn't see Him or know Him. But you do know Him, because He remains with you and will be in you." Jesus refers to the Holy Spirit as another counselor.

The Greek word for counselor is the word *parakletos*. It has many meanings such as helper, comforter, counselor, legal defense, etc. The important thing to take away here is that this noun is only used in regards to a person. Interestingly, the Greek word used for another has two basic meanings in Greek. The first usage connects to the idea of "another of a different kind." This would imply contrast and distinction. The second usage is connected to something or someone of the same kind. In this verse, Jesus is telling His disciples that He is going to have the Father send a counselor of the same kind and nature as Christ Himself.

Up to this point in his ministry, Jesus has been the *parakletos* to His disciples. His time with them is limited because of His approaching assignment on the cross. He knows there will be a separation from them of His physical presence. For this reason, He promises to send another one of the same kind as He is to take His place. This is how He can tell them just a few verses later in this same passage that He will not leave them as orphans. If He had returned to heaven with no ongoing connection between Himself and His disciples, they would have developed an orphan mindset of abandonment, uncertainty, and insecurity. Jesus prevents this from happening by sending the person of the Holy Spirit—a gift from the Father to keep the relationship with the Trinity alive and active.

## understanding the holy spirit

Many Christians today have virtually no concept of the Spirit's ongoing personal involvement in their lives. They live as though Jesus is distant, the Father is removed or absent, and the Holy Spirit is just a symbol. This is a tragedy because such a misunderstanding causes a lack of spiritual vibrancy and vitality in their lives. The ensuing result is that believers feel and act like spiritual orphans, unsure of the Father's will and purpose, disconnected from Christ's truth and grace.

If the Holy Spirit is just a distant, mystical force or abstract symbol of a distant God, then this would make sense. By contrast, if He is the third member of the Trinity actively living inside believers, then no Christian is ever really isolated or alone. The Bible assures us that He is with us and makes the words and presence of Christ a daily reality (John 14:26)! How often, as believers do we need encouragement and direction? How regularly do we need counsel and comfort? Our enemy regularly attacks us with fear and condemnation. If we were spiritual orphans, we would have no chance of surviving. The gospel message is that Jesus not only died in our place, but He also wants to live through our lives in the person of His Spirit. He has provided another counselor like Himself to provide everything we need in our walks with God.

Imagine if Jesus still lived in Jerusalem in the twenty-first century. He would talk with you face-to-face if you could get there to connect with Him. The challenge would be that with more than one billion Christians in the world, His time would be severely limited. At best, He could only afford a few minutes of His busy schedule to interact with you once every decade or so. Nevertheless, who wouldn't want to meet with Jesus face-to-face? Therefore, you'd save up your money for several years, buy an airplane ticket, secure a visa, and make hotel arrangements. While the few minutes you'd spend with Him would be remarkably wonderful, you would be left feeling that you needed ongoing interaction in order to develop a relationship with Him.

Waiting another ten years for your next interaction would seem too long, right? This is exactly why He promised His Holy Spirit! We can have direct access to the throne of God—anywhere and anytime—to receive exactly what we need.

The only way that we can develop this kind of living connection with the Holy Spirit is to recognize that He is a person who desires to speak to us and interact with us. His goal is to reveal Jesus to our hearts. He loves to make a big deal about the perfect Son of God. One of His primary assignments is to remind us of everything that Jesus taught His disciples (John 14:26). As we develop a relationship with the Holy Spirit, we experience all of the benefits of being in a relationship with Jesus. He makes Christ's presence and Word alive inside our hearts as we spend time with Him.

## personal characteristics

I would like to mention three personal characteristics of the Holy Spirit that are revealed in Scripture. These traits remind us of His personality and the fact that He desires to have an ongoing personal relationship with us.

The first one is intellect. We read in 1 Corinthians 2:11 (NIV) that the Spirit has an intellect. "For who knows a person's thoughts except their own spirit within them? In the same way no one knows the thoughts of God except the Spirit of God." An impersonal "it" or "force" would not be able to know and discern the thoughts of God the Father. He is a living person with access not only to both the Father's and Son's inner thoughts, but He also has access to your deepest thoughts! Romans 8:27 (NIV) reminds us that "He who searches our hearts knows the mind of the Spirit, because the Spirit intercedes for the saints in accordance with God's will." Paul is telling us that the Spirit has a mind. He is capable of thinking, analyzing, interacting, and understanding. That is intellect!

Secondly, the Holy Spirit has feelings. Some people get bent out of shape with this idea because they imagine God being stoic and impersonal. Ephesians 4:30 (NIV) instructs believers to be careful how they interact with the Holy Spirit because He is sensitive. "And do not grieve the Holy Spirit of God, with whom you were sealed for the day of redemption." The context of this passage of scripture helps us really understand what is being communicated about the Spirit. In Ephesians 4 the context has to do with immorality—believers not living according to the standards of God's Word. Paul says that any behavior contrary to God's revealed Word grieves or hurts the Holy Spirit.

When we look like the world either through action or speech, it wounds the Holy Spirit. This can be through gossip, lying, slander, deception, pride, or sexual immorality. When we commit sin, we often internally feel conviction, a personal awareness or sensation that something is wrong. This is a really good indication that He is not pleased with our actions. The relationship is damaged, and He wants to bring immediate restoration. Conviction is proof that the Holy Spirit has feelings.

Finally, the Holy Spirit has a clear and specific will. I Corinthians 12:11 (NIV) makes this clear: "All these are the work of one and the same Spirit, and he distributes them to each one, just as he determines." The context of this passage is important because it discusses the role of spiritual gifts among believers. Notice that this verse says that the Spirit gives these gifts as He wills. Since He has a will, He is able to do whatever He deems best based on His personal volition. This is exactly what we see throughout the New Testament. He speaks in Acts 13:2 to launch the ministry of Paul and Barnabas. He testifies of Jesus (John 14:26), He teaches believers what they need to know about Christ (John 14:26), and He convicts people of sin (John 16:8-11). There are many other examples we could look at. The point is that the Holy Spirit has a will that we must be sensitive to seek and obey.

## deepening the relationship

Once we realize that the Holy Spirit has intellect, emotions, and a will, we can appreciate the fullness of this idea of personality. The only way to know Him personally is to understand that He is a person who desires our friendship. Developing a relationship with anyone requires one sure thing—personal interaction.

What does this mean practically speaking? It means that His presence can be welcomed or rejected when we interact with Him. We can acknowledge Him or ignore Him. His presence can be shunned or valued in our lives. And His conviction can be heeded or resisted. In other words, one's relationship with the Spirit is directly affected by his or her daily interactions with Him. Some Christians pray and ask the Lord to speak to them but then refuse to respond to the gentle nudges of the Holy Spirit. Others cry out to know God more fully but ignore the persistent promptings by the person of the Spirit. When they do these things, they are sabotaging the answer to their own prayers!

spending time with God's Holy Spirit, we get to know Him better. He is a person who desires to speak, guide, lead, counsel, comfort, provide, direct, protect, and interact with you! He is available at any moment to speak to you and reveal Jesus and His Word directly to your hungry heart. This is why it's so important to develop a personal relationship with Him. The essence of spiritual growth and development is learning to interact with the Holy Spirit through a strong personal relationship.

# CHAPTER 6

# hearing the holy spirit

**W**hen I look back on my life, I can see the imprint of the voice of the Holy Spirit in significant seasons when He guided me very clearly. Whether it was marrying my wife, Sarah, or stepping into ministry, planting a church, or moving overseas, I attribute all of these key moments to hearing the voice of the Holy Spirit. He is a person who desires to communicate with us. This reliance on His voice started when I was about to graduate from college.

I was praying about what to do next as I had big visions and dreams about what God wanted for my life, and I didn't know what was next. A few days after receiving my degree, I volunteered to help at a basketball camp. One day, one of the coaches asked me what I was going to do next with my life. My response was simple enough.

I said, "I'm not sure, but I'm praying."

Without hesitating, he looked at me and said, "If you are praying, you should be getting an answer." With that, he walked away. His comment stunned me. I had been praying for months with little to no sense of direction.

God used this man's comment to help me realize that I was doing most of the talking in prayer, but I wasn't listening much for the Holy Spirit's response. Amazingly, as I changed my approach, God began to direct me into His purpose within a few short days. He showed me that I had been praying for Him to do what I wanted instead of listening to what He was actually saying. This experience helped me understand that God knows what is best for my life. Even though it wasn't what I thought I should be doing, the next step had been right in front of me the whole time. It was almost so simple I couldn't believe it. Even today, there are things in my life that go back to my obedience in that moment. Far too many people are looking for some new teaching, spiritual insight, or a prophetic word, when the Holy Spirit just wants to show you that what God has planned is right in front of you!

## important decisions

Have you ever had to make an important decision? Maybe it was related to God's best for your future? It could have been something major to do with finances or marriage. It could have been small, like which church to attend or where to go to school. How did you go about making the decision? While we may not understand how to be led by the Spirit when we first come to Christ, the closer we walk with Him, the easier it gets. Being led by the Spirit is vitally important in the twenty-first century—simply because it has always been important. The only way God has directed His people in any church age is through the voice of His Spirit.

My pastor growing up, the late Billy Joe Daugherty, helped me understand this idea. He often talked about learning to hear the voice of God through the Holy Spirit. In other words, the voice of God is discerned through proximity to the Spirit. Oral Roberts, one of Pastor Billy Joe's mentors, used to say that the voice of God is both "the smallest and the loudest voice that you will ever hear." What does he mean? God's voice can be easily missed if we aren't intentional to develop intimacy with the Spirit. However, once we hear His voice, it's so clear that we can't miss it. God speaks to us by His Spirit, and when He does so, His voice is unmistakable.

Acts 8:26 tells us that God gave direction to Philip through an angel. By contrast, in verse 29 of the same passage, we see that the Holy Spirit speaks to Philip. What is amazing about this passage is that both Philip and Luke (the author of Acts) knew the difference between the two. This is important because it shows us that the Spirit has a voice and is intricately involved in leading believers into God's perfect will. Too many people in our generation are looking for external confirmation of God's voice. God always speaks to His people through the pages of Scripture as well as through His Spirit. The Spirit makes the Word come alive in our hearts as He guides us into God's truth (John 16:13). He makes God's Word practical in our lives, so we know how to apply it daily.

I remember feeling slightly nervous about my first driving experience in Australia. I was driving on what felt like the wrong side of the road. Even the steering wheel was on the wrong side of the car. I had no idea of how to get from point A to point B except that the vehicle came equipped with a GPS (Global Positioning System). Amazingly, every time I would make a turn, the electronic voice computer system would route me to my destination with precision. Even when I made a wrong turn, the system would give me new directions until I arrived safely at my intended destination. Did you know that heaven has a GPS for navigating life? The voice of the Spirit is God's Positioning System. The Holy Spirit will keep you in Christ's truth as well as on the right course for fulfilling God's purpose for your life.

## hearing and listening

The verb combination of hearing and listening is referenced over 690 different times in the Bible. This may not seem significant until you recognize that the words praying/talking are only listed 160 times, faith is mentioned a mere 246, and even one of the biggest themes in the Bible—love—gets 496 mentions. All of these concepts are important, but it's obvious that hearing and listening are priorities to God. Hearing and listening are how we receive from Him. Why do I place such an emphasis on this? The reason is that God wouldn't emphasize our responsibility of hearing and listening if He weren't speaking to us. He is speaking; are we listening?

John 10:27 (NIV) presents a great passage in helping us to better understand this idea. Jesus said, "My sheep listen to my voice; I know them, and they follow me." Sometimes sheep are characterized as being dumb animals, but in reality, they are highly intelligent in the area of voice recognition. Sheep know their shepherd's voice and will instinctively follow it. Likewise, they will not listen to someone they don't know, no matter how hard that person may try to entice them away from the shepherd. Jesus then goes on to say that He knows His sheep. Please don't overthink this. The clear message is that if you are a believer in Christ, then He knows you and subsequently knows how to speak to you through His Spirit in a way that will move you to follow Him.

I've heard many Christians say that God doesn't speak to them. This simply isn't the case. If you belong to Him, then I can guarantee that He is speaking to you! Often we don't slow down long enough to listen for what He is saying at this moment or to take inventory of what He has already said to us because we think it is too basic or that we have already mastered it. What I have found is that what the Spirit is saying now is what the Spirit has always been saying. The Spirit is at work confirming God's purposes to our hearts. Our responsibility is to lean into what He is communicating to us. Let me ask you this simple question: What is God teaching you in this season by His Spirit? Take a moment and write some thoughts down, even if it seems basic. Even simple things that He has already communicated will combat any notion that He no longer speaks to you!

I think it's similar to our modern voice recognition technology. We have everything from Siri on our smartphones to Alexa on cloud-based Amazon devices that now respond to us with some version of "Go ahead. I'm listening." Likewise, I believe the Holy Spirit speaks to each of us by name. He says, "Caleb," and my responsibility is to respond, "I'm listening to you, Holy Spirit." Just this simple act of recognition prepares our hearts to receive what He desires to communicate to us.

## possible obstacles

My desire is to make this as practical as possible because living without an awareness of the Spirit's voice makes Christianity really difficult—especially in the twenty-first century. Since we have scriptural promises and assurances that God desires to communicate with us, what do we do if we aren't hearing His voice? Let's examine a few obstacles that could be impeding one's capacity to hear His voice.

The first obstacle that we have already identified is that we aren't listening. This may seem obvious, but we need to realize that the Spirit doesn't want to compete with the voices of the world to get our attention. Did you know that listening requires at least three key components? These are stillness, focus, and responsiveness.

Many believers have so many other voices competing for their attention that they can't distinguish between the Spirit's voice and ambient noise. Being alone with God to be quiet and still in His presence is essential if we are to be exposed to the Spirit's voice.

Another factor to consider is focus. I love sports. After I married my beautiful wife, I would have the TV on silent so that I could listen to her talk while still watching my favorite game. The problem was that even without the volume on, I was still more focused on the sporting event than on her voice. I quickly discovered that this was disastrous for our marriage because I was too distracted to really hear what she was saying. I had to turn off the TV in order to listen to her voice; yet, there was still one more challenge to overcome—sometimes I didn't want to hear what she was saying! Many Christians approach the Spirit's voice in the same way; they are willing to listen as long as He tells them what they want to hear. Being led by the Spirit requires us to be still, focused *and* responsive!

The second obstacle is a lack of trust. Many believers want to follow God's way if it is easy, involves no risk, and doesn't require any inconvenience. This will never work. Philip was called to leave a thriving revival in Samaria to go into the wilderness. It didn't make any sense naturally, but it was the Spirit's leading. Proverbs 3:5-6 (NIV) reminds us, "Trust in the Lord with all your heart, and lean not on your own understanding, in all your ways acknowledge Him, and He will make your paths straight." Trust is vital if we are going to hear from heaven. In fact, the more trust we extend in His direction, the more understanding the Spirit sends our way.

The final obstacle in hearing the voice of the Spirit is not walking in obedience to God. Isaiah 59:2 states, "Your iniquities have separated you from (the voice of) God." What does this verse mean? It's difficult to hear God's voice when unconfessed sin, guilt, and offense have taken root in our lives. If you are in this condition right now, the Lord is speaking clearly over life, "Repent, and put me first again." In so doing, you will hear the voice of the Spirit clearly again.

What if we aren't hearing God's voice clearly? Ask yourself the questions, "Am I really listening to God, trusting God, and obeying God?" If not, then you have the opportunity right now to change this reality and ask the Spirit to help you listen, trust, and repent. If you do, you will hear His voice more clearly every day. You will quickly discover that He has been waiting to communicate with you regularly.

## how does he speak?

I remember when the Spirit started speaking to me about moving my family to another country. I felt some initial shock at the idea but also a lot of peace and excitement. I have learned that the Spirit will lead you in the big details as well as the small. How does He do this? The first and most important way He leads us is through His Word. Psalms 119:105 (NIV) states, "Your word is a lamp unto my feet and a light unto my path!" His Word reveals His will for our lives, and it is full of promises that can be received by faith and become evident in our lives. We have the opportunity every day to hear directly from heaven. As we spend time in the Word, He promises to illuminate our steps.

The second way is the still small voice. In this chapter, we have talked about the Spirit's voice, but we haven't described it. When the Spirit told Philip to run beside the Ethiopian eunuch who was riding in his chariot, what did His voice sound like? In 1 Kings 19:11-12 (KJV), God is trying to speak to the prophet, Elijah. The story records that there is a wind, an earthquake, and a fire, but God isn't in any of these. Instead, He speaks through a "still small voice." This is still how the Spirit speaks to us today—in a still small voice in our spirits!

Many people ask me how to learn to hear this still small voice better. My response is usually pretty simple—the more time you spend with someone, the more familiar you become in recognizing that person's voice! Many people can recognize who is calling them just by hearing the person's voice saying "hello" over the line. How can that be? They spend time with someone and no longer need him or her to say, "This is so-and-so." I believe the voice of the Spirit sounds like an internal cell phone call.

Lastly, the voice of the Spirit is confirmed to us through people. Sometimes it may be a prophetic word from another believer, or it could be through a sermon or a book or a small group meeting. The key is that what is being communicated must line up with what the Word of God already tells us. It needs to bear witness to what the Spirit is telling your spirit. For example, have you ever been in a service or read a book and all of a sudden, some word or phrase seems to come alive and resonate with you? In that moment, you knew that God was saying something just for you! What is that? That is the Spirit speaking to you through other people! It is confirmed by His peace in your heart.

One afternoon, when I was in college, I was walking to the cafeteria, and I bumped into one of my theology professors. Much like the coach in the story I shared at the beginning of this chapter, he asked me what the Lord was speaking to me. I didn't know how to respond and said something about being done with my math class and heading to the cafeteria to eat. He looked at me and said, "He's probably speaking. Maybe you're just not listening?" How often do we fail to recognize what He is speaking to us at this moment because we are too preoccupied with other interests? The Holy Spirit's voice is a still small voice that will always lead you into God's perfect will. Through practice and exposure, you will be able to trust Him to always lead you, guide you. The more you spend time in His presence, the more you will be able to discern His voice speaking to you.

CHAPTER 7

# the
# gifts
# of the
# spirit

I have learned that there is no distance between God and His people when we operate in the gifts of the Spirit. I think of a specific church service I attended while on a mission trip to the nation of Honduras. I was seated in the crowd as my pastor finished preaching and started praying for healing at the close of the service. Some ten thousand people filled every corner of the room. As the ministry time started, I walked to the back of the room. It was so packed that people couldn't get to the front. I was a young man eager to see how God moved in corporate settings like this one.

At the back of the room, my eyes landed on a lady with a large tumor on the side of her neck. My spirit was moved with compassion to pray for her. I found a translator so that she could participate in the prayer for healing. Almost as soon as we started praying, this huge lump dissolved and disappeared. This precious woman started screaming in Spanish, "I am healed. I am healed." There was no microphone in front of her or me, no stage, no camera, and no lights. Just a heart-felt hunger for God's presence, and God healed her right there on the spot. This is what the gifts of the Spirit are about. They are for everyday usage so that any believer can be the hands and feet of Jesus.

I think of a blind lady in Mexico several years ago. It was one of my first trips to Mexico, and I was leading a group of middle school teenagers on their first missions trip. We were sharing

Jesus' love in a slum area on the US-Mexico border. We decided to share the gospel message in her tiny shack with only one room. As we communicated the good news, an older lady in the room, who was also blind, listened intently. One of the family members asked us to pray for this blind woman. I asked one of the fourteen-year-old girls with us to lay hands on her and pray for her. The power of the Holy Spirit filled that tiny room and restored the blind lady's sight instantly. As I look back, I think about how an unknown person in an unknown place received total healing because of the operation of the Spirit's gifts.

One of the critical functions of the Holy Spirit is to equip believers with the gifts necessary to advance the gospel and to build the church. By church, I am not talking about the four walls of a building or a particular denomination, but rather the people Jesus is building to be the Spirit's abiding place in this generation. Of course, when people are edified, the structure of the church can also expand, but we must never get the one ahead of the other. A solid spiritual infrastructure in people's lives requires the Holy Spirit's work in order to produce something of lasting value. This is where the gifts of the Spirit come into operation—they are the means of releasing the Spirit's power into people's hearts and minds. And where the Spirit is moving, there will always be a revelation of the person of Jesus (John 16:13).

Jesus has graciously released spiritual gifts through His Spirit to every believer. Notice what Paul says in 1 Corinthians 12:4 and 7 (NIV), "There are different kinds of gifts, but the same Spirit. . . . Now to each one the manifestation of the Spirit is given for the common good." This passage is important for three reasons:

First, it tells us that all spiritual gifts have the same source, the Holy Spirit. Second, this passage tells us that the Spirit manifests these gifts in the lives of all believers. Third, the gifts of the Spirit aren't given for personal benefit or applause but for the benefit of others. This can be summarized as follows: The Holy Spirit gives various gifts to every Christ-follower to be used to build up others. An understanding of this idea is fundamental for anyone to be able to mature in his or her relationship with the Holy Spirit.

## manifesting gifts

Sadly, many Christ-followers don't really have a clear picture of what the gifts of the Spirit look like. Paul continues in 1 Corinthians 12 to elaborate on this and as how they operate in our lives. "To one there is given through the Spirit the message of wisdom, to another the message of knowledge by means of the same Spirit, to another faith by the same Spirit, to another gifts of healing by that one Spirit, to another miraculous powers, to another prophecy, to another distinguishing between spirits, to another speaking in different kinds of tongues, and to still another the interpretation of tongues. All these are the work of one and the same Spirit, and he gives them to each one, just as he determines" (1 Corinthians 12:5-11, NIV). What does this passage tell us about a person's relationship with the Holy Spirit?

Paul is saying that the Spirit doesn't just come to give us some kind of abstract spiritual experience or empowerment. Instead, He releases specific gifts into our lives. There are nine of them outlined in this passage of scripture. Many people refer to these gifts as the manifestation gifts of the Spirit. Let's look at them briefly:

- The first one is the *word of wisdom*. This is supernatural insight into how to practically proceed in a difficult situation. Often the situation is complex or convoluted. Often the word of wisdom is expressed as a practical step or a direction a person needs to take that will produce a clear resolution to a problem.

- The second one is the *word of knowledge*. The Spirit gives us understanding and revelation into matters that there is no way we would have known about otherwise. This happens when people know something by the Spirit that they didn't learn by using their natural senses. For example, "Someone has a back issue, and the Lord is going to heal you." In this case, it's the word of knowledge coupled with the gift of healing because at that moment, the person is given awareness of someone's back condition as well as God's desire to heal it.

- The *gift of faith* is the capacity to believe God in the midst of difficult or even impossible circumstances. An example of this would be the ability to believe God for financial provision when there seems to be no human way for those finances to materialize. It's an inner confidence to believe God even when circumstances may be saying the exact opposite.

- The *gift of healing* is the operation of the Spirit to release a specific area of healing in a person's life. This can be either physical or emotional in nature. This could look like an anointing to heal specific disorders such as cancers, see physical deformities restored, or resolve specific emotional bondages and wounds by the Spirit's power.

- The *working of miraculous powers* is the ability to see super-natural signs and wonders happening with the purpose of confirming the gospel and facilitating the advancement of God's kingdom. This could be the raising of a dead person, stilling a storm, or releasing rain in the face of an ongoing drought. Next is *prophecy*. This has to do with Spirit-empowered speech that provides exhortation, edification, and comfort. It confirms God's purposes and direction in a person's life. It is a direct word from God to encourage a person concerning a current or future situation. It releases God's perspective about a person's life.
- The *distinguishing of spirits* is the ability to discern the source of the operation of a spiritual reality in someone's life. Obviously, all spiritual power only has one of two sources. This gift identifies the source as well as the goal or plan of the source.
- The *gift of tongues* is an inspired message in a heavenly language—unknown to people—that contains specific instruction for a group of believers. This is often released in a corporate assembly of believers in the presence of the gift of interpretation.
- The *interpretation* of tongues is the ability to translate a message in tongues into the language spoken by the group of believers. This could be English, French, Spanish, or some other known language so that those present understand what God is saying through the heavenly tongue.

## ministry gifts

Besides manifestation gifts, the Bible also describes two other categories of spiritual gifts the Holy Spirit releases in our lives. The first category is found in Ephesians 4:11, where Paul describes five ministry gifts available for the church. These five gifts are essential for the operation and function of the church. They are identified as follows:

- **Apostle:** This comes from the Greek word meaning a messenger sent forth with orders to accomplish a specific mission. Hence, some people see missionaries as the modern-day equivalent of apostles because they go into foreign nations for the advancement of the gospel. In a broader sense, though, apostles are those gifted by the Spirit to take new ground for the kingdom in any of the seven spheres that we talked about in the chapter on the Spirit's purpose. This can look like new strategies, ideas, or influence within a specific sphere.

- **Prophet:** The prophet exhorts, encourages, and consoles other believers to strengthen them in their faith. The prophet regularly operates within the gift of prophecy that we have already talked about, but often this ministry gift isn't directed towards a specific individual. Instead, prophets have the ability to encourage believers to new levels of commitment and consecration to Christ and His work.

- **Evangelist:** This is someone who devotes him or herself to proclaiming the gospel and leading people to Jesus. This ministry gift is usually evident because a large number of people respond to the gospel through this person's ministry.

- **Pastor:** This is probably the ministry gift that we are most familiar with in the twenty-first century. This person is the shepherd of a local group of believers responsible for leading and guiding them into the truths of the Christian faith.
- **Teacher:** Finally, the fifth ministry gift is identified as one who preaches and teaches the principles of the Christian faith in a simple, concise way. People are able to grasp spiritual truths and concepts through this gift. Even difficult theological concepts are articulated in a way that others can understand.

It is important to mention that the ministry gifts can overlap in someone's life. This means that a pastor may be a teacher of the Word of God, or an evangelist may have a prophet's gifting to exhort and console, or a teacher may also be highly effective as an evangelist or prophet. Finally, I think it's important to realize that at no point in the New Testament does Scripture tell us that the ministry gift of the apostle has been done away with. Sadly, there is much abuse regarding the gifting of the apostle in our generation. Many want to say it no longer exists; others claim that they are apostles because they place the term on a business card or a sign outside the church doors. Both fall short of what the Bible teaches.

A true apostle usually operates in multiple ministry gifts simultaneously. This is necessary in order to launch new initiatives in the kingdom by taking ground for Christ. For this reason they often face more than usual spiritual resistance and often experience suffering. Apostles often start a work in the kingdom and then mobilize others to take it over before moving on to the next endeavor. In other words, apostles lay the foundation for a work before turning it over to others to continue building the work.

## motivational gifts

The final list we want to consider is found in Romans 12:6-8, where Paul identifies seven other gifts often referred to as motivational gifts. Most of these gifts are natural to a person's disposition and God-given talents. The seven are listed as follows:

- **Prophecy:** This gift encourages, exhorts, or comforts other believers with direct words from God.
- **Serving:** Since there are many gifts associated with serving, this gift describes a wide variety of gifts where believers serve others. This includes everything from gifts of hospitality to a natural inclination to take care of others' needs practically.
- **Teaching:** This gift set communicates and articulates the Word of God in a way that others can understand. It requires a clear understanding of God's Word and character.
- **Exhortation:** This is the ability to motivate other believers to patient endurance, brotherly love, and good works. This is more than encouragement. It's encouragement that results in ongoing action.
- **Giving:** This is the gift of sharing one's possessions with others. All Christians should be givers, but those with this gift go above and beyond what is normal or expected in Scripture. They feel a motivation to give generously to advance the gospel and take care of others.

- **Leadership:** This gift speaks of the various leadership functions necessary in the church for implementing and accomplishing the Spirit's purposes for His people.
- **Mercy:** This gift usually takes the form of serving others in the name of Christ during difficult times. Often believers will demonstrate this through visitation in the hospital or prison, prayer, and acts of compassion.

It is also important to remember that nowhere does the Bible tell us that these are the only gifts the Spirit gives to God's people. Rather, these are a sampling of the more prominent ones necessary for Christ-followers' development. The key point to take away regarding all three categories of gifts is this: Since the Spirit operates in all believers, each believer can be assured that he or she will have at least one of the gifts in operation in his or her life. Yet, I have never met a believer with only one gift! Do you know what your gifts are? If not, it is important to pray and ask the Spirit for insight about this matter. Taking a spiritual gift test or inventory can also be helpful.

Finally, did you also know that it's possible to receive new spiritual gifts? Paul makes this clear in 1 Corinthians 14:1 when he makes this amazing statement: "Follow the way of love and eagerly desire gifts of the Spirit, especially prophecy." Do you see what he is saying? Hunger for the operation of the Spirit in your life will lead to new spiritual gifts being deposited inside of you. This is so encouraging to me because it tells me that we don't have to be stagnant in our expression of the Spirit's power. He always has new dimensions for us to grow into as we learn to be more useful in our service towards others. I believe that all

Christians can have gifts from all three categories in operation in their lives—manifestation, ministry and/or motivational gifts, all at the same time.

## purpose of the gifts

We have already mentioned the purpose of the gifts of the Spirit. However, I think it's important that we reemphasize that the Bible says that these gifts are given for the common good. The idea is that the various giftings are never to be used for personal exaltation or recognition. Rather, the idea is that the Spirit wants us to operate in the gifts He has given us in order to serve others and glorify Jesus. Nothing is more powerful than when Jesus receives glory, and His church is strengthened and expanded. Why mention all of this again? There is much at stake in using our spiritual gifts in the right way.

Regretfully, some people have used the gifts for self-promotion and to draw attention to themselves. This is the opposite of why the Spirit releases the gifts in our lives. Always remember that His goal is to magnify and exalt Jesus. When the spotlight is put on both the gifts and the person operating in the gifts, it's impossible to magnify Jesus. Every time Jesus is removed from the spotlight, things will not end well (Isaiah 46:8). In the previous generation, much harm was done in the body of Christ when the focus was removed from Jesus. Judgment soon followed. We must not make the same mistake in the twenty-first century. Always remember that the Holy Spirit gives us gifts to glorify Jesus!

One of the Greek words Paul uses for the gifts in 1 Corinthians 12 is *charisma*. This word derives from the root word *charis,* meaning grace. This is the same word that describes how every believer has received salvation in Jesus Christ: by grace. In other words, we don't earn our salvation any more than we earn the gifts. Can you imagine people boasting about how they were able to save themselves from hell and forgive their own sins? That would be ridiculous. Likewise, the gifts of the Spirit are never to be used to build a name, a reputation, or a social-media following. They are to be used to edify the body of Christ and glorify Jesus.

## the operation of the gifts

How does a believer exercise the gift(s) of the Spirit? 1 Corinthians 12 deals primarily with how the manifestation gifts are to be activated and exercised in the life of a believer. Paul tells us that these gifts come by one and the same Spirit. This means that it is the Holy Spirit who activates these gifts inside of us and then teaches us how to exercise them. If you have the Spirit in your life, then you have access to the gifts. And every Christian has the Spirit living inside of him or her (Romans 8:9).

This is where the baptism in the Spirit is so crucial. We will talk about this more in a later chapter. For now, it is enough to say that once a Christian experiences the baptism of the Holy Spirit, the gifts are fully activated. It's similar to a bank card that a financial institution sends your way. In many countries of the world, the card won't be activated until the individual verifies his or her identity with the bank. Once this crucial step is accomplished, the person receives access to everything in the bank account. If you don't activate the card, then it's possible to carry a piece of plastic in your wallet with no value to you or others. Spiritually speaking, many Christians have heaven's bank card, the Holy Spirit, living inside of them, but until they receive the fullness of the Spirit, many of the gifts lie dormant inside of them.

The empowerment of the Spirit not only activates the gifts, but it also gives us courage for exercising the gifts. Stepping out in some of the more prolific gifts can be daunting. Releasing words of knowledge, prophetic insight, or a gift of healing requires confidence in God. This is where the Holy Spirit helps us to begin exercising these gifts. I like using the term "exercising" the gifts because it is similar to working out. If you don't use a particular muscle, it will become weak and unable to resist any weight. For example, the more I exercise the prophetic gift in my life, the more accurate it will become. In the same way, we must exercise our spiritual gifts with the Spirit's courage. This will strengthen our spiritual muscles so that we can be greater blessings to others.

I remember the first time God used me in the gift of healing. I was in a special service at Oral Roberts University. The president of the university asked the students to raise their hands if they needed healing of any kind in their bodies. A young man raised his hand next to me. I found out later that he had intense pain in his lower back. I laid my hands on him and started praying. He started screaming, "It's hot! It's hot!" God had healed him immediately! He proceeded to go forward and testify in front of everyone that Jesus had healed him when I placed my hands on his back. I was as amazed as he was.

As we have already seen, these gifts are for the common good. This means that the expression of these gifts will happen in the presence of other believers and for the benefit of others. We have to take a step of faith to be willing to exercise our gifts around others. This is challenging, especially in any Christian context where people value performance. Performance places pressure on people to use their gifts in a certain way. Please note that Paul never puts pressure on the believer—he places the pressure on the Spirit.

A spiritual gift is not a performance; it's a service to the body of Christ. This means that it is okay to be you when you exercise your spiritual gift. You don't have to copy other believers or use fancy, spiritual language. Remember that the gift isn't for you. It's for other people. Ask the Lord to give you confidence and compassion to share your gifts with others. Also, remember that exercising the gifts brings Jesus pleasure. Ask the Spirit to use you to glorify Jesus as you step out!

Practically speaking, in order for people to grow in their gift-ings, they have to create opportunities for both mentorship and practice. Believers that operate in a particular gift need to help others grow and develop in that same gift. Since spiritual gifts are like muscles, we need to exercise them individually as well as in the presence of people who are stronger in an area than we are. Often it is through much practice in a safe context that believers become confident in the operation of the gift(s) in their lives.

For example, the word of knowledge is powerful and can set people free when used correctly. A younger believer felt prompted to use this gift during a time of prayer in the church. He shared the word with another believer who was more seasoned in delivering words of knowledge; this believer immediately discerned that the word wasn't for him. Rather, it was for a brother standing right next to him in the meeting who was going through some challenges that the younger believer couldn't have known about. The word was one hundred percent accurate. It was just delivered to the wrong person. Rather than judge the younger believer or try to shut down the operation of this gift, the more seasoned believer encouraged him to keep developing greater accuracy.

Finally, much of the operation of the Spirit is based on individual hunger. In 1 Corinthians 14:1, Paul instructs believers to eagerly desire spiritual gifts and especially the gift of prophecy. This tells us that much of the operation of the gifts of the Spirit depends on our desire to be used by God to minister to others. Jesus tells His disciples in Matthew 5:6 (NIV) that hunger is a law of the kingdom of God. "Blessed are the hungry for they will be filled." The Spirit always responds to spiritual hunger. Pursuing the person of the Spirit actually releases a spiritual hunger inside of us for Jesus to be glorified. As we pursue this hunger to be used by Him, you will be amazed at the gifts He starts to release in your life to fulfill this desire.

Let's close this chapter with another good example to help us understand this whole idea of the operation of spiritual gifts. It's like a house that has various electrical appliances such as a stove, a fridge, a microwave, lamps, etc., but no electricity is connected. None of these appliances benefit the people living in the house even though they are all present. If the homeowner desires electricity, he or she will find a way to get it turned on. Once the electricity is activated, everything in the house becomes fully functional. Yet, electrical current doesn't mean that you automatically know how to use your oven to bake a chocolate cake. It will take practice as well as someone else's coaching and skill to make a delicious dessert. In the same way, the baptism of the Spirit activates the gifts, gives us a hunger for the gifts, and releases the courage necessary to exercise the various gifts.

The gifts of the Spirit are available for every believer. You already have at least one in your life due to the fact that you have the Spirit in your life as a Christian. Ask the Holy Spirit to show you which ones He desires you to operate in. Seek these gifts through prayer, and operate in them for Christ's glory and the benefit of other believers.

# CHAPTER 8

# the character of the spirit

I f the Holy Spirit is in you and is empowering you, then there should be some kind of evidence or fruit in your life. This is important in order to bring balance to the whole idea of spiritual gifts. During a church service not long after I had decided to fully surrender my life to Jesus, my pastor suddenly looked at me and said, "Come up here on the stage and share how the Holy Spirit took your cusser away." There were two challenges with this request.

First, I had never shared my testimony in this setting before, and the very thought of doing so terrified me. I knew that the Holy Spirit was working powerfully in my life, but I wasn't open about the specifics with other people. Secondly, I had no idea how the pastor knew that I had such a foul mouth and liked to cuss so freely.

I was sitting towards the front of the building, so I knew that he was talking directly to me. Honestly, I hadn't even realized that my tendency to use curse words could have an effect on my walk with Jesus. As I walked to the stage, I understood that the work of the Holy Spirit in my life was to make me more like Jesus. As I shared my testimony of how I had fully surrendered my life to Jesus a few weeks previously, I received insight into the Holy Spirit's work happening in me even in that very moment. He did something powerful in my character, changing and conforming me to the image of Christ. After that moment, I didn't have to consciously hold back certain thoughts or words anymore. I was different—changed, with no desire to even say those things anymore.

When you surrender yourself to the Spirit, there is a renewal process that occurs, allowing you to be transformed into Christ's image. You can think differently. You can act differently. And you can speak differently. It was no longer about my ability or personal resolve not to do something. Instead, it was the Spirit's power living inside of me that produced the difference. Please understand that the Holy Spirit isn't just for a church service or a revival service or a supernatural moment. He is not sent so that we can operate in spiritual gifts and then go back to "normal life." Rather, the Holy Spirit is sent to live inside of us for day-to-day living. When we talk about His character, we are talking about surrendering ourselves to what He wants to do inside of us. We call this the fruit of the Spirit, which is the result of the character of the Spirit manifesting inside of us.

The work of the Holy Spirit in our lives is not just external; it is also profoundly internal. We have spent considerable time talking about the external work of the Holy Spirit. He empowers God's people to reach the world by giving them bold witness, gifts of the Spirit, and hearts to serve others. All of this is essential for God's kingdom to advance in our generation with power, but what is even more essential is the inner work of the Spirit in our lives. What He desires to accomplish in our lives is equally as wonderful as what He desires to accomplish through our lives.

Paul goes to great lengths to establish this idea in Galatians 5:22-25. This passage is often referred to as the fruit of the Spirit because it describes the results of what a life possessed by the Spirit looks like. This passage states: "But the fruit of the Spirit is love, joy, peace, forbearance, kindness, goodness, faithfulness, gentleness and self-control. Against such things there is no law. Those who belong to Christ Jesus have crucified the flesh with its passions and desires. Since we live by the Spirit, let us keep in step with the Spirit." In order to understand this passage, we have to first remember that we are all created in the image of God.

This concept is often referred to as the *Imago Dei*. This is the Latin expression for Image of God. Basically, it means that each life has value, worth, and purpose because every single human being is created in God's image. God's image is stamped on each person's life. No matter how marred or stained someone's life may be because of sin, he or she is still loved and valuable in God's sight. Though sin can never erase the external *Imago Dei*, it has created a breach of the internal *Imago Dei*. Paul describes this reality in Romans 3:23, where he tells us that "All have sinned and have fallen short of the glory of God." What is God's glory? Is it not His image? His character? And His integrity all combined into this one idea?

Since we have all fallen short, we have all failed to bear the *Imago Dei* in our hearts. Sin has polluted His reflection in our hearts and ultimately destroyed our relationship with the God of glory. This is why Jesus came! He forgives us and restores our relationships with the Father. This is what makes the gospel such good news: We now have access to God's glory again through the Person of the Holy Spirit. The Holy Spirit is holy because God is holy. One of His primary goals in our lives is to make us holy. He does this by establishing the character of Christ within us. Paul refers to this character as the fruit of the Spirit. It is the reflection of Christ's character inside of us, the inner *Imago Dei*. Believers increasingly express God's character as they grow deeper in their relationships with the Spirit.

## God's holiness

Before we discuss the specifics of the fruit of the Spirit, it's important to remember the "who" from this passage in Galatians chapter 5, the Holy Spirit. Hopefully, you've figured out by now that this book is all about Him. The name of the third member of the Trinity is interesting because it comprises two words—holy and spirit. Simply stated, this tells us that He is the Spirit of God and as such His nature is holy. Let me give you an example. My full name is Caleb Wehrli. What if you said to me, "I like your first name, Caleb. However, you really need to change your last name to something easier to pronounce." I would respond that my name is an integral part of who I am. In the same way, we can't pick and choose what part of the Holy Spirit we want based on our preferences. His name is Holy Spirit. While you may be thinking that is really basic, please understand that His name is incredibly significant. Why so?

The word holy describes the essential character of God (1 Peter 1:16). It means that He is set apart and altogether different. It also means that He is of absolute value and beauty while still remaining accessible. No wonder God's Spirit possesses the very quality that most distinguishes God as God. Sadly, in some contexts, people have portrayed holiness as legalism—a list of spiritual dos and don'ts. Such a definition makes holiness undesirable and causes people to reject the concept of holiness. However, this is nothing short of a lie from hell. God is infinitely valuable and eternally desirable.

The four living creatures encircle God's throne, crying out in praise, "Holy, holy, holy" (Revelation 4:6). It is interesting that the Bible specifically says they never stop. As they go around the throne, they see a fresh aspect of His holiness and are so moved that they cry out in adoration again, "Holy, holy, holy." The point is simply that true holiness is attractive, not repulsive. Holiness is so attractive in fact that no one in heaven seems to be able to get past it in the book of Revelation. Paul is saying to us that the Holy Spirit wants to manifest this aspect of God's character inside of us. He takes the character of God and forms it in us so that we will be set apart and consecrated for His purposes.

So what does God's holiness look like in the life of a believer? It looks like God's character being formed inside of people using the imagery of fruit. Paul gives us a list of various characteristics the Spirit produces in us to help us understand this complex idea. There are nine *fruit* of the Spirit presented as essential aspects of His character. Please note that the use of the word fruit in the singular is intentional. You may be thinking to yourself, "*Shouldn't it be fruits of the Spirit, i.e. in the plural?*" The answer is that the Greek text uses the singular neuter case. Why would this be? The Spirit only produces one kind of fruit in us, holiness. Yet, it has nine aspects or expressions that help us better understand what holiness looks like practically in the twenty-first century.

## holiness and the fruit

How does the Spirit establish His character in our lives? Galatians 5 gives us some insight into this matter. Paul indicates that the Holy Spirit makes us holy by producing fruit in our lives. The agricultural metaphor of fruit gives us a picture of sweetness and desirability. Have you ever tasted a fresh mango from East Africa? Or a banana fresh from the tree in South America? Or blueberries straight off the bush during the summer in the northern part of the United States? They are so delicious that all you can think about is eating more. This is the imagery being developed here for us in this passage. The nine aspects of this one fruit of holiness are so attractive and so desirable that our responses should be those of gratitude that God's own Spirit would be committed to producing these inside of us. In all sincerity, we could make each one of these aspects an entire chapter in this book. By way of summary, here is a quick overview of the list:

- **Love:** The divinely empowered ability to love God and His people (John 13:34), love seeks the highest good of another person without motive for personal gain.
- **Joy:** This is the ability to find delight and gladness in God and His promises even in difficult situations (Philippians 4:4).
- **Peace:** The ability to trust God in the midst of difficult situations and circumstances produces rest for our hearts and minds based on the knowledge that He is in control. His peace protects us from worry, fear, and anxiety (2 Corinthians 13:11b).

- **Patience:** This is the capacity to endure difficult circumstances while trusting God to confirm His promises (Ephesians 4:2).
- **Kindness:** This is the expression of God's goodness towards other people. Goodness and kindness are closely connected (Ephesians 4:32). Kindness is goodness in action directed towards those around us.
- **Goodness:** This attribute is a zeal for God's truth and righteousness expressed through our lives through acts of kindness (1 Timothy 3:3 and Luke 7:37-50).
- **Faithfulness:** This ability to be reliable and trustworthy as a follower of Christ due to an unswerving loyalty to Jesus requires submission and obedience to the Spirit (Revelation 2:10).
- **Gentleness:** This characteristic is closely linked to humility. It is strength under control (Ephesians 4:2). Gentleness allows us to be angry when anger is appropriate and submissive when submission is needed.
- **Self-control:** This is the ability to master every issue of our lives under the leadership and direction of the Spirit. This requires ongoing submission and surrender of our lives to Him (2 Peter 1:6).

All of these characteristics together form the character or fruit of the Spirit. As we deepen our relationships with Him, we have the assurance that He will give us the power that we need to develop and manifest His holy character.

## character development

Perhaps in reading through these nine characteristics, you have identified one or more areas in your life that lack the Spirit's character. This list in Galatians chapter 5 is very useful for evaluating our spiritual lives and character. None of us are perfect, and as we grow in our walks with the Spirit we will be increasingly sensitive to His voice. One of the areas where the Spirit loves to work is in personal character formation. He desires us to be conformed to the image of Christ (Romans 8:29). He wants our lives to look like Jesus. What an awesome thought!

When we determine that there are cracks in our character that the Spirit is identifying, it is essential to address the matter immediately. This is one of the marks of genuine Christian maturity. Please remember that He doesn't point out our inconsistencies in order to make us feel bad about ourselves. That would be harsh and critical. Rather, He does this to call us higher so that we can be conformed to Christ's image! How do you respond when He starts talking to you about an area of your life that needs some work?

In this same passage, Paul shows us the Biblical pattern for cooperating with the Spirit in character development. He says, "Those who belong to Christ Jesus have crucified the flesh with its passions and desires" (Galatians 5:24, ESV). Who belongs to Christ? Anyone, anywhere, who has placed his or her faith in Jesus now belongs to Him. Notice that it is the responsibility of every Christ-follower to do something decisive with the passions of the flesh. We are called to crucify them. This is not Jesus' responsibility; it is ours. Everyone has passions and desires that wage war inside of them (James 4:1). If we follow these passions and desires, we will thwart the character of Christ that the Spirit is trying to establish inside of us.

When this happens, we begin to operate in the flesh. In the verses immediately preceding the passage that identifies the fruit of the Spirit, Paul contrasts them with what could be called the fruit of the flesh. It's quite a list: jealousy, fits of rage, selfish ambition, sexual immorality, impurity, debauchery, dissensions, factions, envy, drunkenness, orgies and the like (Galatians 5:20-21, NIV). When he says, "and the like," it reminds us that this list is not comprehensive; he's just giving us some examples. Reviewing this list is really useful in determining whether we are living in the Spirit or walking in the flesh. Paul concludes by saying that anyone who walks in the flesh will not inherit the kingdom of God (Galatians 5:21).

We know that Paul is writing to believers. He is basically telling both the believers of his generation as well as those of us alive in the twenty-first century that there are only two possibilities when it comes to spiritual focus. We are either in the Spirit or in the flesh. How tragic to think that some believers would start off in the truth of salvation but fail to inherit any portion of God's kingdom because they didn't allow the Spirit to produce the character of Christ inside of them. This is why Paul says that there is only one solution to ensure that the passions and desires of the flesh don't spoil the character of Christ inside of you—crucify them!

Isn't this at the heart of the gospel message? Jesus told His followers while on earth that if they wanted to be His disciples, they had to take up their crosses and follow him (Matthew 16:24).

Taking up the cross doesn't mean putting on a nice piece of jewelry that represents the Christian faith. No! It means cruci-fying any passions and desires that are contrary to Christ and His kingdom by the help of the Spirit. Someone once said, "If we don't kill sin, sin will eventually kill us." This is Paul's compelling argument in Galatians 5.

He is showing believers the danger of the flesh while at the same time reminding us that we are not powerless, helpless victims. We have the Spirit of God working inside of us! His holi-ness is attractive and desirable. He is committed to producing the character of Christ on the inside of us. Our responsibility isn't to make this happen in our own strength; we are called to partner with Him in this process. As we are diligent in surren-dering our sinful desires, He will be faithful to release a greater fullness of fruit, and our characters will be more consistent with that of Christ's.

You are called to exhibit Christ's character in a wicked and perverse generation (Philippians 2:15). This looks like the Spirit producing fruit in your life. He gives us the power that we need to kill sinful passions and desires that could sabotage Christ's character being formed within us.

# CHAPTER 9

# encountering the holy spirit

**A**s a pastor and a church leader, I have seen firsthand how the Holy Spirit transforms peoples' lives on a regular basis. This transformation involves the gifts of the Spirit, the character of the Spirit, and the purpose of the Spirit. All of these areas demand that we encounter the Spirit for ourselves! I remember one Sunday morning in particular when I decided to preach on the Holy Spirit and how to encounter Him personally. There was a lady who had grown up Catholic who started attending our church a few weeks earlier. The first Sunday this lady visited, she realized she already had religion, and she made a decision to surrender her life to the Lord. The next Sunday, she decided to be baptized in water in obedience to Christ's command. The next week, as I shared about encountering the fullness of the Holy Spirit, her heart was moved, and she decided to respond at the altar to receive everything God wanted to give her.

I prayed a very simple prayer for those responding to the message that morning, and almost immediately, this particular woman felt God's presence fall on her. She began praying quietly in her prayer language. Supernatural joy came over her, and she kept telling people around her, "I keep feeling the presence of His Spirit as joy, peace, and love on the inside of me in a way I have never felt before." She's still in the church today and has since led most of her immediate family members to Jesus, including her grandkids and adult children.

Over the past twenty-five years, as I have traveled across this globe from country to country, I have seen the Holy Spirit do similar things. Where He is invited, He shows up and fills believers with the power to live for Jesus. It doesn't matter a person's background, age, demographic, or denominational affiliation; He is available to those who ask.

Sadly, there is much controversy, debate, and misunderstanding that surrounds the person of the Holy Spirit and His ongoing work in the lives of believers. Some have even used the Bible to try and legitimize the idea that the work of the Spirit stopped after the early disciples. This idea is sometimes referred to as cessationism. It comes from the English verb "to cease." The good news is that the Holy Spirit's supernatural power and presence haven't ceased or been hindered by some people's faulty interpretation of Scripture. More than 650 million people globally are experiencing the daily reality of the Holy Spirit! Others reject the idea of cessationism but are still unsure what the Bible says about receiving the Holy Spirit.

I would like us to take the blank page approach to this subject. Regardless of what you have been taught or what others have said to you about it, let's start afresh and allow the Bible to speak for itself. This is important because it gives the Holy Spirit the opportunity to give you new insight into His power that is available for your life today. Acts chapter 19 is a really good place to examine the importance of encountering the Holy Spirit. "While Apollos was at Corinth, Paul took the road through the interior and arrived at Ephesus. There he found some disciples and asked them, 'Did you receive the Holy Spirit when you believed?' They answered, 'No, we have not even heard that there is a Holy Spirit'" (Acts 19:1-2, NIV).

This passage takes place at least twenty-five years after the outpouring of the Spirit in Acts 2 on the Day of Pentecost. This is significant because it shows us that the empowerment of the Holy Spirit is a multigenerational experience. What do I mean? Note that all of the main characters in Acts 19 are absent from the Acts 2 outpouring. Neither Paul nor the disciples in Ephesus were even Christians twenty-five years earlier when the Spirit fell in Jerusalem. In other words, this is an entirely new generation of disciples being exposed to the reality of the Holy Spirit. What's the point? Some people say that the Day of Pentecost in Acts chapter 2 is a stand-alone Holy Spirit event—occurring at a precise historical moment, never to be repeated again in the history of the Church. The only problem with such an argument is that Acts 19 occurs decades after Pentecost within the context of an entirely new faith community.

This passage is also significant because, in Ephesus, Paul meets a group referred to as disciples. Interestingly, the term disciples is only used in the New Testament for people who already have a personal relationship with Jesus. This means they have placed their faith in Christ and are born again. Notice that Paul doesn't celebrate the status of their conversion; instead he asks them a direct question: "Did you receive the Holy Spirit when you believed?" (Acts 19:2, NIV). Paul's question is important. He is referring to being baptized in the Holy Spirit, a second and subsequent work of the Spirit following His initial work of salvation. Clearly, believers have the Holy Spirit at conversion (Romans 8:9). So if they are already believers, why is Paul asking them if they have received the Spirit? The best way to answer this question is to explore what the Bible says about Spirit baptism.

## baptism in the bible

The word baptism means to immerse or submerge. In the New Testament, we see three different kinds of baptism. The first kind of baptism is recorded in 1 Corinthians 12:13. Paul, the principal character in the Acts 19 narrative, tells us "For we were all baptized by one Spirit into one body." Notice who does the action in this verse; it is the Holy Spirit. We are baptized by the Spirit into the body of Christ. "You are all sons of God through faith in Christ Jesus, for all of you who were baptized into Christ have clothed yourselves with Christ" (Galatians 3:26-27, ESV). This baptism refers to what we call salvation or being born again which is only possible as the Holy Spirit draws us to Jesus!

The Holy Spirit is within us when we get saved so that we can have a relationship with the Father and experience Christ's grace (Romans 8:15). When you asked Jesus to be your Lord and Savior, you received membership into Christ's body. As powerful as this experience is in the life of a believer, it is not the same thing as being baptized in the Spirit, which we will talk about in a moment. In other words, there's a baptism by the Spirit into the body of Christ during salvation that seals a person's eternal destination, but the baptism in the Spirit is another baptism that allows us to live full of the Spirit's power here on earth.

The second baptism is the most common in the church—water baptism (Matthew 28:19). Water baptism is an outward sign of the inward work of the Spirit of God in your life through salvation. It is publicly declaring to the world that you have been born again. Being baptized in water announces a personal commitment to embrace the first baptism into the body of Christ. If you are born again and haven't been baptized in water, I want to encourage you to take this important step in your walk with Christ.

The third baptism is the baptism in the Spirit. Jesus baptizes us into the fullness of the Spirit's power. Paul, the primary theologian of the New Testament, knew full well that in order to be a disciple of Christ a person must be born again, right? After all, He wrote Romans 8:15 and 1 Corinthians 12:13, which we just examined. As such, his question in Acts 19:2 wouldn't make any sense if he were referring to salvation. If you don't believe me, let's reimagine the conversation together again.

Paul: "Hey, Ephesian disciples, have you received the Holy Spirit? Oh wait, I forgot, you

already have the Holy Spirit because He came when you got saved. . . ."

Some people use this very argument to say that Paul's question proves that the Ephesians weren't Christians yet. However, remember that the word disciple is only ever used in the context of a person who has a personal relationship with Jesus. So what exactly is Paul asking? In short, he wanted to know if they had received the power of the Spirit as the disciples did on the Day of

Pentecost. He had in mind a second and subsequent encounter with the Holy Spirit.

Some people say that the first and third baptisms are the same, i.e., *by* the Spirit and *in* the Spirit are one and the same experience, but this is not the case.

Let's look at another analogy to clear up this confusion. If John pours water on his son's head and then John's brother, Uncle Peter, pours water on the same boy's head, we wouldn't say that this is the same event, would we? Likewise, when the Holy Spirit baptizes us into Jesus (the first baptism), it's different from when Jesus baptizes us into the Holy Spirit (the third baptism). Another useful analogy is to think about an empty bottle being filled with water (first baptism), and then you decide to throw that same full water bottle into a larger body of water (third baptism). I hope you can see that being baptized in the Bible has three different contexts.

1 John 5:7-8 (NKJV) offers us further insight into the three baptisms. It says, "For there are three that bear witness in heaven: the Father, the Word, and the Holy Spirit; and these three are one. And there are three that bear witness on earth: the Spirit, the water, and the blood; and these three agree as one." The first part of the verse describes the Trinity bearing witness to the truth. The Father, the Word and the Spirit are in total agreement. Their witness is in heaven. Then there are three that bear witness on earth: the Spirit, corresponding to the baptism of the Spirit, the water representing water baptism, and the blood indicating being baptized into the body of Christ. When someone

experiences the three earthly witnesses. they are unwavering in their faith regarding the three witnesses in heaven.

## paul's question

Let's return to Paul's question: "Have you received the baptism of the Spirit?" Unfortunately, some believers are uncomfortable talking about the third baptism. The main objection they raise is along the lines of why a believer would need such an experience. The reason is that God designed you to live not only a Spirit-redeemed life but also a Spirit-empowered life. The church was never intended to operate in its own strength or cleverness or strategy. Instead, God has called you and me to operate in the power of the Spirit as His witnesses (Acts 1:8). Paul wanted to make sure that the disciples in Ephesus experienced the fullness of this power.

It is increasingly difficult to be a witness in our world. There are pressures on every side to silence the name and person of Christ. This is why Jesus wants to supply us with the power we need to be bold witnesses for Him while living victorious Christian lives. It's possible to grow up in a Christian home, attend church regularly, and even attend different conferences, yet still not walk in the fullness of the Spirit's power. How will you know when you experience the fullness of the Spirit? Personally, I sensed a boldness that I had never known previously, and I received my heavenly prayer language. My life was changed forever. Likewise, you will know. Imagine if you put your finger in an electrical socket. How do you know when your body interacts with the electricity in the wall? You will know it, I guarantee it!

Please understand that being baptized in the Spirit doesn't make you better than other believers. Some Christians act superior when they experience the Holy Spirit's empowerment. They have missed the whole point! In fact, pride and conceit are contrary to the character of the Holy Spirit. What is the benefit of being baptized in the Spirit? It will make you a better version of you—empowered to reach the world around you. If God has supernatural power available for you, wouldn't you want to receive it? Remember again that Jesus needed the baptism of the Holy Spirit for His ministry (Luke 3). If this is true for Him, don't you think it would be true for you as well?

CHAPTER 10

# experiencing
# spirit
# baptism

119

I still remember my first experience with the Holy Spirit, the third baptism that we discussed in the previous chapter. It happened while riding in the car with my parents after a Sunday evening church service. The pastor had preached about the Holy Spirit that evening, talking about His person and His gifts. My parents started asking my brother and sister about the message as they discussed some of the ideas. I finally decided to ask some questions of my own because my heart had also been deeply stirred. My parents encouraged me that even as a child, I could receive the power of the Holy Spirit.

Bowing my head in the car as we sped down the highway, I asked for the gift of the Holy Spirit. My parents agreed in prayer with me. At that moment, I felt the power of His presence course through my body, and I began to speak in an unknown prayer language (tongue) for much of the journey back to our house. This experience left an indelible mark on my heart. I knew the Holy Spirit was real and wanted to fill me with His presence. As we surrender to Him daily, the gift of the Holy Spirit makes God's presence very close and personal, and it's available for everyone—even children.

Many believers have tried to discredit themselves from receiving the fullness of the Spirit due to one reason or another in their background. Some people think they don't know enough about the Holy Spirit. Others think they haven't heard enough information about Him. The truth is that the Holy Spirit responds to child-like faith! Jesus told us that the kingdom could only be received through simple faith (Mark 10:15). This is also true for experiencing the Holy Spirit. We don't need great theological insight or spiritual intensity. We just need to understand God's simple promises about the Holy Spirit and respond with a desire to be filled. Remember, He shows up where He is invited. When we want Him, He comes. When we position Him in the right place, He can move in our lives and baptize us in His power.

The Bible doesn't always use the term Spirit baptism to refer to a second experience (third baptism) with the Holy Spirit for spiritual empowerment. The baptism of the Spirit is also described in the Bible as the gift of the Father (Acts 2:38 and 1:4), the promise of the Father (Luke 24:49), being filled with the Spirit (Acts 2:4), the reception of the Spirit's power (Acts 1:8), the Spirit coming on people (Acts 8:16), and the outpouring of the Spirit (Acts 2:44-45). All of these ideas refer to one and the same experience. I like to use all of them as a definition for being baptized in the Spirit. What is Spirit baptism? It's our Heavenly Father's promise that we receive as a gift when the Holy Spirit is poured out over our lives, and we are filled with His power.

## subsequent experiences with the holy spirit

With such a variety of available terms for the same experience, it is important to understand that the Bible describes Spirit baptism in multiple ways and contexts. In the previous chapter, we already talked about the Ephesian believers in Acts 19 who had not received the baptism of the Spirit. We also discussed the 120 believers on the Day of Pentecost. In both cases, all the disciples in these stories were already Christians (see John 20:22). This means they had already received the Spirit as an inner witness of the guarantee of salvation (first baptism). Yet, in both cases, they received a second and subsequent experience of the Holy Spirit's power.

Another great example is found in Acts chapter 8. Philip goes to Samaria to preach the Word of God. God confirms his message with signs and wonders. The Bible says that many people responded to the gospel message, including a sorcerer named Simon. Act 8:13 states that Simon believed and was baptized. What does this mean? This isn't a trick question. Obviously, it would mean that Simon is now considered a Christian at this point. The next two verses detail the apostles coming to Samaria to pray for these new believers. What were they praying for them about? Luke tells us, "That they might receive the Holy Spirit because the Holy Spirit had not yet come on any of them; they had simply been baptized in the name of the Lord Jesus" (Acts 8:16, NIV). Clearly, Peter and John wouldn't have needed to go to Samaria if the believers were already walking in the fullness of the Spirit after salvation.

Another good example is Acts 9. Saul, the persecutor of the church, had a powerful encounter with Jesus on the road to Damascus. He loses his physical sight during the encounter but receives spiritual insight that Jesus is the one he has been persecuting. He enters Damascus to seek the Lord concerning what he should do with his life now that he has become a Christian. Ananias is sent by the Lord to help the new believer. When he arrives, he places his hands on Saul and says, "Brother Saul, the Lord—Jesus, who appeared to you on the road as you were coming here—has sent me so that you may see again and be filled with the Holy Spirit" (Acts 9:17, NIV).

Wait! Didn't Paul receive the Holy Spirit when he encountered Jesus on the road to Damascus? Yes, that is when he surrendered control to Christ. In fact, he is the one who would later write that in order to be a Christian, the Holy Spirit must live inside of you (Romans 8:16). So what is going on here? Ananias knew that there was a subsequent encounter with the Spirit's fullness that Paul would need for ministry. His mission that day was to ensure that Paul would receive the fulfillment of everything that Jesus died to release in his life. The passage says nothing about tongues, but we do know that Paul boasted to the Corinthians that he prayed in tongues more than all of them (1 Corinthians 14:18). So why didn't Luke include tongues when he talked about Paul's conversion in Acts 9?

I believe the best answer is two-fold. First, he had already established a pattern in the book of Acts for what happened when someone was filled with the Holy Spirit—they received a heavenly prayer language (Acts 2, Acts 10, and Acts 19). Secondly, it demonstrated the correct emphasis in seeking the Spirit's fullness in our lives. We pursue Him. We desire to encounter His fullness and power. We hunger and thirst for everything that He desires to release in our lives. The evidence of that encounter follows, but it is never our primary focus. Paul received the fullness of the Holy Spirit with His heavenly prayer language, but the emphasis is on the person of the Holy Spirit and not the manifestation of the Spirit.

## objections

There are various objections to baptism in the Spirit. Probably the biggest question people have concerning the baptism of the Spirit is confusion between salvation and ministry empowerment. Many people say, "I thought I received the Holy Spirit when I was born again. So I need to be baptized in the Spirit?" I have already mentioned this in the previous chapter, but the answer to this question is a resounding, "Yes!" You received the Spirit when you accepted Jesus as your Lord and Savior (conversion). Paul addressed this in Romans 8:9 (NIV): "You, however, are not in the realm of the flesh but are in the realm of the Spirit, if indeed the Spirit of God lives in you. And if anyone does not have the Spirit of Christ, they do not belong to Christ."

Notice what Paul is saying: The Spirit lives inside of everyone who has accepted Jesus as their Savior. Again in verse 16 (NIV) he states, "The Spirit himself testifies with our spirit that we are God's children." The only way that we know that we are born again is that the Holy Spirit provides evidence of the inner trans-formation that has occurred. If someone doesn't have the Spirit then he or she is not a Christian. If you have received Jesus as your Lord and Savior, then you have also received the Holy Spirit, but this doesn't mean that you have been baptized in the Holy Spirit.

Another major objection is when people say that Spirit empowerment is not for today. They believe it was only for the early disciples in Acts chapter 2. As we have already seen from Acts 19, Paul expected believers to receive Spirit baptism even decades after the initial outpouring. This is consistent with Peter's promise to the onlookers on the Day of Pentecost, where he states, "The promise is for you and your children and for all who are far off, for all whom the Lord our God will call" (Acts 2:39, NIV).

What promise is he talking about? The promise of the Father is the baptism in the Holy Spirit (Luke 24:49). The crowd present in Jerusalem on the Day of Pentecost is the 'you' Peter is addressing. Their children would be the next generation of believers (like the ones we read about in Acts 19). And all who are far off refers to future generations of believers like you and me.

For others, the obstacle is that they think the baptism of the Spirit is strange. This is especially the case when it comes to discussing the heavenly prayer language, sometimes referred to as tongues.

Different languages are only strange within a monolinguistic context. In many parts of the world, people regularly speak two or three languages connected to various ethnic groups. Why would it be strange for the Spirit to give us a special heavenly prayer language? I like the example from my friend Stephen Kuert. He is an American born in Kenya to missionary parents. He speaks fluent Swahili. Often, after he has preached in the United States, people from East Africa will talk to him in order to test his capacity in Swahili.

As they chat in Swahili, Stephen is reminded of many things: the beautiful country of Kenya where he grew up, the wonderful people who are some of his best friends, the gracious Kenyan hospitality, and many other things about this amazing country. He doesn't think, *This is so strange. Don't these people know that we are in America and that we should only speak English here.* The reason is that the Swahili language connects him to a land far away where he has deep roots. In the same way, praying in your heavenly prayer language connects you to a heavenly dimension, the culture of heaven, even though you are currently still here on this earth.

The final obstacle I will mention is that people often tell me that the baptism of the Spirit isn't for everyone. They will often mention 1 Corinthians 12:27-30, where Paul says that not everyone receives the gift of tongues. Paul is discussing one of the specific manifestation gifts necessary for edifying the body of Christ. In other words, this specific gift is to be used for corporate edification. The manifestation gift of tongues is for sharing a divinely inspired message in conjunction with the gift of interpretation for a group of believers. The outcome of such an operation of the Spirit is that the body is edified.

By contrast, speaking in another tongue, given as a personal prayer language, is used for personal edification. In other words, the manifestation gift of tongues for select believers is different from the personal prayer language of tongues that all believers can receive to amplify their prayer lives. How do we know? Praying in tongues for personal edification does not require interpretation, although it can certainly be profitable. Furthermore, using your prayer language isn't for the benefit of anyone else—it's communication between you and heaven. This is why Paul can say in I Corinthians 14:18, "I thank God that I pray in tongues more than all of you." He is talking about his personal prayer life and how much praying in tongues enriched it.

Finally, at no point in the New Testament does Scripture record believers not receiving their personal prayer language when the Spirit filled them. In Acts 2, the passage indicates that all 120 began to pray in tongues. In Acts 19, all of the Ephesian believers present began to pray in tongues. Likewise, in Acts 10, all of those present in Cornelius's house began to pray in tongues when the Holy Spirit came upon them. This is why those accompanying Peter were so shocked: the Gentiles had received the Spirit in the same way the Jews had on Pentecost (Acts 10:46)

## receiving the baptism of the spirit

Let's close this chapter with some practical steps you can take in order to receive this amazing experience with the Holy Spirit. The first is to remove all barriers in your life. For many Christians, this includes any past misinformation about the Holy Spirit that is contrary to what the scriptures teach. This is one of the main purposes of this book—to help you get a clear picture of what God's Word says about Him. Beyond a faulty misconception of who He, is there can also be unresolved areas of sin and unforgiveness that need to be made right (Acts 2:38-39).

Secondly, you need to request the gift of the Holy Spirit. Yes, the Holy Spirit is a gift. "If you then, though you are evil, know how to give good gifts to your children, how much more will your Father in heaven give the Holy Spirit to those who ask him!" (Luke 11:13, NIV) Our Father loves to give the gift of the Holy Spirit just as He loves to give the gift of His Son's salvation. Have you asked Him for this gift?

Thirdly, you need to receive baptism in the Spirit by faith. Some people say that this is too difficult, but I don't think that this is the case. For example, did the Father force you to get saved? No. How do we receive Jesus as our Lord and Savior? We do so by faith (Ephesians 2:8-9). Likewise, we receive the Holy Spirit by faith. Remember Hebrews 11:6 reminds us that without faith, it's impossible to please God. Without faith it's also impossible to receive the fullness of the Spirit in our lives.

Finally, you need to relate to the Holy Spirit every day. Just as we understand the importance of going to the gym and exercising regularly in order to produce overall health and wellness, we need to be diligent spiritually. After I received the Spirit by faith, I received my heavenly prayer language. Over the years, I have exercised this gift by praying in this prayer language daily. This is one of the main ways God empowers us and strengthens us to live this Christian life.

Please remember that the Holy Spirit already lives inside of you if you are born again. This idea causes problems for many Christians because they don't understand how the Spirit can be inside of them without their having received the fullness of the baptism of the Spirit. One of the best illustrations we can use comes from East Africa. In that area of the world, visitors often show up unannounced. Sometimes they will enter someone else's home without anyone actually inviting them inside. In that culture, it is rude not to officially welcome the guest by shaking his or her hand.

Often a guest has to sit in the living room for some time prior to being officially welcomed by a member of the family. Once a family member walks into the living room, they are expected to say, "Karibu," (Swahili for you are welcome) and shake the guest's hand. This constitutes an official welcome. Likewise, all Christians have a guest in the person of the Holy Spirit residing in the living room of their hearts. Yet, often he has never been officially welcomed or allowed to manifest the fullness of why He came into their hearts in the first place. It is not just for salvation; it is also for empowerment to live this Christian life in Christ's victory!

CHAPTER 11

# discovering the spirit

I n this book so far, we have talked about one central theme—
the Holy Spirit and His role in our lives in the twenty-first century. Sadly, for many believers, He is nothing more than a
theological idea or doctrinal position from the pages of some
old denominational book. This is tragic because the Holy Spirit
was never intended to be God in the past, but God in the now.
He is holy God—in action, right here, and right now. And He
wants to be active today in both your life and mine. The main
reason for this book isn't to impress with you how much I know or
depress you by how little I don't know about the Spirit. No way!
The purpose of this book is to challenge you with the simple
question Paul asked the Ephesians in Acts 19:2 (NIV): "Have you
received the Holy Spirit since you believed?"

Have you experienced the fire of the Holy Spirit burning in
your heart? Has your life been marked by His ongoing presence
and power? Are you walking in His fullness to be a bold witness
of Jesus on a daily basis? Are you exhibiting His character and
personality? Do you know the intimacy of being saturated in His
presence? Is He manifesting His gifts through you to glorify Jesus
and serve others? If not, then this chapter is for you!

We have to move from the theoretical to the practical. As
Christians we are called to keep living out the book of Acts
in our generation. In the twenty-first century, we are in Acts
chapters 29, 30, 31, and counting. What do I mean? Nowhere

in the Bible do we read that the Holy Spirit came to earth with fire, power, and glory for the first decade or two of the early church . . . before deciding that He had worked hard enough at accomplishing heaven's plan . . . and then deciding to retire to turn the Father's business over to future disciples.

Aren't you glad that at the end of Acts chapter 28, there isn't an addendum with a subtitle that reads: "The Holy Spirit Returns to Heaven"? Can you imagine the implications that would have on our world and especially on the Church? Could you imagine how devastating this information would have been to those early disciples and Paul? Let's imagine Paul having just such a fictitious conversation with the Holy Spirit.

Paul: "Holy Spirit, we are seeing the gospel spread throughout the world like never before!"

Holy Spirit: "True, it's been an amazing start for the Church."

Paul: "Yeah, it has! Entire cities have been turned upside down like Ephesus and Philippi, and now—even in Rome—the gospel has reached Caesar's palace."

Holy Spirit: "These decades have been great, but I'm homesick for heaven."

Paul: "I mean, there have been miracles and signs and wonders and incredible deliverances. . . ."Holy Spirit: "I think it's time for me to return to the Father."

Paul: "And priests, and prisoners, and jail wardens, and prominent politicians have all surrendered their lives to Jesus because of your anointing. . . ."Holy Spirit: "Paul, are you listening to what I am saying?"

Paul: "What?! There are still entire nations and regions of the world that have never heard the message!" Holy Spirit: "Oh, I'm sure you will manage just fine without my power and presence."

To me, the saddest part about this totally fictitious and potentially heretical conversation is that many Christians live as though the Holy Spirit actually departed and went back to heaven at the end of Acts. Are you one of those? Are you trying to live out Jesus' mission and calling using your own strength and ability? The message of this book is simple: The Holy Spirit is still willing and available to fill you with the same power and fire that He demonstrated in the early church for the simple reason that He hasn't gone anywhere! He's still here—very much alive and working in our midst. And He wants to empower you to be His hands and feet in the twenty-first century. What exactly will this look like in your life?

In *Empowered*, we have explored several aspects of what the Spirit's presence and power look like in our lives. Let's take a quick review before we close this chapter.

**The Spirit in the 21st Century:** The Holy Spirit gives us everything we need to make Jesus real in any situation. He is available even during the spiritual emergencies of the twenty-first century.

**The Arrival of the Holy Spirit:** The Holy Spirit shows up where He is invited, and when He shows up things, always change. He showed up on the Day of Pentecost, and He hasn't stopped showing up since. He wants to empower us to fulfill Jesus' mission of reaching the world.

**Purpose of the Holy Spirit:** The purpose of the Holy Spirit is to fulfill the plan of God to change the world. He does that by empowering us to be His witnesses. We fulfill His mission by starting right where we are and receiving His heart for the world around us.

**The Person of the Holy Spirit:** The Holy Spirit is a real person ready to make the presence of Jesus alive inside of you today. He is the Third Person of the Trinity who wants a personal relationship with you.

**The Personality of the Holy Spirit:** The Holy Spirit wants ongoing personal involvement in your life. He wants an intimate relationship with you. You are invited to know Him personally!

**Hearing the Holy Spirit:** The Holy Spirit has a voice and is committed to helping every believer walk in God's perfect will. One of the greatest joys of developing a relationship with the Holy Spirit is that He will lead you into God's perfect plan for your life. He is speaking to every believer. We must tune in to His voice so we can hear and obey what He is saying to us.

**The Gifts of the Spirit:** There is no distance between God and people when they operate in the gifts of the Spirit. The Spirit wants to be active in your life by releasing the ministry, manifestation, and motivational gifts in and through your life. Today is a great day to receive His gifts.

**The Character of the Spirit:** The evidence of the Spirit's empowerment in your life is that there will be fruit. You are called to exhibit the Spirit's character by abiding in Him. The flesh and the spirit are in a perpetual battle. The Spirit gives us the power to demonstrate the character of Christ and defeat the flesh.

**Encountering the Holy Spirit:** The Holy Spirit fills us when we get saved so that we can have a relationship with the Father and experience Christ's grace. Yet, God designed you to live not only a Spirit-redeemed life, but also a Spirit-empowered life. He wants to empower you to be a witness for Jesus.

**Experiencing Spirit baptism:** The baptism of the Spirit is available for everyone. This includes you! There are several steps we can take to partner with Him in this regard. The first is to remove all barriers in your life. Secondly, request the gift of the Holy Spirit. Thirdly, open your heart by faith. Finally, ask Him to fill you every day.

In summary, when we experience the Holy Spirit in His fullness, we will experience all of these concepts as well as many others that we haven't even looked at in this book. He is an inexhaustible source of everything that we need in our lives: peace, joy, strength, boldness, direction, wisdom, power, intimacy, freedom, inspiration, humility, passion, confidence, and character.

Where do we go from here? Back to where we started this chapter—discovery. I want you to discover the Holy Spirit for yourself, every day. How does this happen? If you haven't received the baptism of the Spirit yet, then I want to encourage you to do the following: Ask Him to fill you! Invite the Holy Spirit to saturate your life right now. Let Him touch you in a fresh and new way. Whatever area of deficit you are experiencing in your life or difficulty you are currently facing, the Holy Spirit wants to give you the direction, power, and strength for what you need. The Bible says that our Father will give the gift of the Holy Spirit to those who ask (Luke 11:13). So, ask with faith, knowing that this is a promise from God for you!

As you discover the Holy Spirit, I am confident that your life is going to be used in significant ways to make Jesus known in our world. Remember that the Spirit's purpose, person, and power all point to knowing Jesus and making Him known! There is no greater discovery possible than to experience the ongoing revelation of Jesus in and through your life.